WHY *Jesus* MATTERS

WHY *Jesus* MATTERS

The ETERNAL IMPACT *of* ONE EXTRAORDINARY LIFE

BRUCE BICKEL *and* STAN JANTZ

BARBOUR
PUBLISHING

ISBN 1-59310-019-1

Published by Barbour Publishing, Inc., P.O. Box 719, Uhrichsville, Ohio 44683 www.barbourbooks.com

Our mission is to publish and distribute inspirational products offering exceptional value and biblical encouragement to the masses.

ecpa Member of the
Evangelical Christian
Publishers Association

Printed in the United States of America.
5 4 3 2 1

TABLE OF CONTENTS

WHY *JESUS* MATTERS AT ALL. . .

INTRODUCTION

Jesus is the most important figure in human history, and he is also the most controversial. Does that surprise you? It might if you see Jesus as a quiet, gentle man who taught us how to love our neighbors and forgive our enemies. But if you know Jesus as a revolutionary person who turned the world upside down, then you probably agree with us.

The popularity of Jesus during his life on earth is without dispute. During his thirty-three years, Jesus was known by everybody from kings to beggars. Even though he never had more than a few dozen true followers, crowds of many thousands would routinely gather to hear him speak. Once when he was standing on the shore of a lake, a mass of humanity pushed him to the water's edge. He had no choice but to get into a boat to get away from the people who longed for a glimpse, a word, or perhaps even a touch from this man from Galilee.

That Jesus was controversial is also a matter of record. On the one hand, he was a champion of the poor, the meek, and the oppressed. On the other hand, he challenged the religious leaders, calling them snakes and hypocrites. After three years of this, they finally had enough of his insolence and sentenced Jesus to death. The religious leaders couldn't do the deed, however, so they enlisted the aid of the Roman government, which carried out his execution just to keep the peace. They hung Jesus on a cross, which ever since has stood as a symbol for Christianity, the belief system founded on the person and work of Jesus Christ.

Three days after his execution, the Bible and history record that Jesus rose from the dead, and forty days after that he ascended into heaven, gone but not forgotten. As popular and controversial as Jesus had been while he was living on earth, it was nothing compared to what would happen after he returned to his heavenly home.

The controversy started immediately with the resurrection. Even though there were more than five hundred eyewitnesses who saw Jesus in the weeks after his death, the critics planted seeds of doubt. He hadn't really died but merely fainted, they said. They questioned his teachings, the miracles, and his ability to prophesy. The followers of Christ did their part to tell the truth about Jesus as they carried out his command to take the Good

News of his life throughout the world. But one by one many were arrested, imprisoned, and put to death for their faith in the one they called Savior and Lord.

And that's the way it's been in the two thousand years since Jesus visited this planet. His followers have spread the news about the love and forgiveness of Jesus, while many scholars and those in authority have done their best to discount, discredit, and destroy the message. We're twenty centuries removed from the actual life of Jesus on earth, so you would think that the critics and the controversy would die down. But if anything the criticism has intensified, because Jesus and his teachings and claims continue to impact every area of life.

Jesus has had a huge effect on history, culture, and science. Through the centuries, no other person or subject has had a greater impact on the arts than Jesus.

The principles Jesus taught and the life he lived have set the standard for ethics and morality. Jesus dramatically changed and improved human relationships, and he redefined what it means to love.

Finally, Jesus brought a new dimension to the life and death issues of faith and belief. He didn't just point the way to God. Jesus claimed to *be* God. In no uncertain terms, Jesus said he was the only way for humankind to escape spiritual death and inherit eternal life.

When you consider all of this—and you will as you read this book—you can see why Jesus still matters in our world. In fact, he matters more today than ever before.

Of course, it doesn't matter what *we* think or write. What matters is *you*. What do you think of Jesus? And does it really matter to you? Does *Jesus* matter to you? Our hope is that this book will encourage you to think about the most important issues of life as you learn more about the most important person who ever lived.

PART ONE

But when the right time came, God sent his Son.

—PAUL THE APOSTLE[1]

Why Jesus Matters in History

More books have been written, more songs have been composed, and more lives have been given in the name of Jesus Christ than of any other person who ever lived. The beginning of his life on earth was the beginning of our calendar, and the end of his life on earth was the most dramatic event in history. Even though Jesus left this world nearly two thousand years ago, more than two billion people living today identify with him in one way or another by calling themselves *Christians*. By all measurements, Jesus is the central figure of the human race.

All this from someone who was born in a small town in the Middle East and lived an uneventful life as a carpenter until he was thirty years old. Only then did he announce to the people around him that he was the Son of God who came to give eternal life to all who believe in him.[2]

Rather than embracing him wholeheartedly (you would think people would do that to the Son of God), many people—especially the religious leaders—were skeptical of Jesus and his incredible claims. They were outraged at what he said and did. How could a *man* be the Son of God? What made him think he could forgive sins?[3] And even more incredibly, how could this man Jesus call himself God?[4]

It was more than the religious and political leaders could tolerate, so they put Jesus to death on a cross. They thought this would silence Jesus and his followers for good.

But when Jesus came back to life after lying dead in a tomb for three days, the story of Jesus and what he taught came alive, too. From that resurrection day to the present day, history has not been the same. You could even say that without the life, the death, and the resurrection of Jesus on this planet, there would be no history, at least not the history we know.

"What do you mean, 'If I can'?" Jesus asked. "Anything is possible if a person believes."

—Jesus[5]

CHAPTER I

THE HISTORICAL JESUS

*E*ven though Jesus is the most influential person who ever lived, many people doubt that he did everything the Bible says he did. They question the virgin birth, they doubt the miracles of Jesus, and most of all, they can't believe the Resurrection. What about you? Do you believe that Jesus was simply a great prophet and a wise teacher, but not much more? Do you have questions about his miraculous life and his claims to be God?

It's okay to have doubts and questions about Jesus. God isn't going to strike you with a lightning bolt from heaven just because you wonder if everything you know about Jesus is true. Jesus invites your doubts and your questions. Remember Thomas, one of the twelve disciples? He doubted that Jesus was alive after the Romans had put him to death on a cross. The other disciples said, "We have seen the Lord!" But Thomas replied, "I won't believe it unless I see the nail wounds in his hands, put my fingers into them, and place my hand into the wound in his side."[6] Thomas wanted proof that Jesus was alive. He wanted to see the evidence.

About a week later Jesus appeared to his disciples and spoke directly to Thomas. Rather than reprimand Thomas for his doubts, Jesus invited the astonished disciple to put his finger into his hands and to put his hand into his side. "Don't be faithless any longer," Jesus told Thomas. "Believe!"[7]

That's the way Jesus always responds to anyone with doubts about his existence and his purpose for entering human history. Like he said to Thomas, he is saying to you, "See for yourself! The evidence is there. I am alive and I am everything I said I was!"

Now, we can't put our fingers into the hand of Jesus, nor can we place our hands in his side, but we can see the evidence from history that Jesus lived and walked this earth. We also can know from the eyewitnesses who wrote about their encounters with Jesus that he healed the sick, raised the dead, calmed the seas, and came back from the dead.

There are few historians who would deny that Jesus lived. The simple fact is that there is more and better historical evidence for the existence of Jesus than any other religious leader who ever lived. In fact, there is more proof for the life of Jesus on earth than any other historical figure living at the time of

Jesus, and that includes the rulers of the Roman Empire. And we don't just have to rely on the Bible for evidence. Roman historians such as Cornelius Tacitus and Suetonius, as well as Jewish historians like Josephus, wrote about Jesus and the people and events surrounding his life.

As for the Bible, the four independent biographies of Jesus were written by four people—Matthew, Mark, Luke, and John—who never contradicted each other in their portrayals of Jesus. These historical documents, collectively called the *Gospels,* are some of the most reliable documents of antiquity.

So we know Jesus lived and walked the earth. What about all of the supernatural things he did? What about the miracles and the Resurrection? Besides the evidence of eyewitnesses recorded by the four biographers, we have the evidence from the lives of those who followed Jesus and gave their lives for him long after Jesus ascended into heaven.

Of the twelve disciples, all but one were killed for their belief in Jesus. Why would anyone give his life for something he knows is a lie? If they did not truly believe that Jesus was God in human form, capable of defying natural laws and able to forgive sins, they would not have died for him. And it wasn't just the people who knew Jesus in the flesh. Why would countless numbers of people through the centuries—including some of the smartest and most respected men and women of their time—die for their faith in Jesus rather than deny that he lived and died and rose again? The answer is that they believed in the person and work of Jesus.

The truth is that Jesus existed and influenced history for good because of the way he lived, because of the love he showed, and because of the life he gave for all people for all time. All Jesus asks is that we believe. As he told doubting Thomas, "You believe because you have seen me. Blessed are those who haven't seen me and believe anyway."[8]

Thinking About Why Jesus Matters

- Would it make any difference to you if the historical evidence regarding Jesus was weak? Would you still believe in Jesus even if there were no proof for what he did and how he lived? Why or why not?

- Imagine you were living at the time Jesus walked the earth. What would have convinced you that Jesus was the Son of God?

- It's one thing to believe that Jesus actually lived. It's quite another to believe in what he said.

I doubt if there is in the world a single problem,
whether social, political, or economic,
which would not find ready solution if
men and nations would rule their lives
according to the plain teaching
of the Sermon on the Mount.

—FRANKLIN D. ROOSEVELT

CHAPTER 2

CIVILIZATION

*T*he statement "Jesus changed the course of civilization" generates no controversy. It is an accepted fact. Billions of Christ-followers who have lived through the centuries since Jesus' time affirm this. But you would expect it from *them*. How about an assessment from the opponents and critics of Jesus Christ? Interestingly, you won't get any argument from them, either.

Jesus' universal impact on our civilization is so obvious that even his antagonists admit the fact. While they don't view his influence as beneficial, they are compelled to acknowledge the fact that he is the pivotal person of history. For example, the nineteenth-century atheist philosopher Friederich Nietzsche considered Jesus to be like poison in society. But by lamenting that the Christ-virus had infected the whole world, Nietzsche implicitly conceded the universal impact of Jesus.

You don't have to be on either of the extreme ends of the "Jesus spectrum" to recognize how he has changed society. Any objective observer would reach this inevitable conclusion simply by looking at a calendar. The entire world marks the passing of time by reference to his birth. Anything that happened before his birth is dated in years B.C. (before Christ). Conversely, events happening after his birth are referenced in years labeled A.D. (*Anno Domini*, from the Latin meaning "in the year of our Lord").

On a personal level, you probably categorize events in world history by reference to your birthday (as in "the attack on Pearl Harbor happened before I was born" or "I was twelve years old when John Lennon was shot" or "I got married at the age of twenty-six"). Measuring personal matters from your birth date is logical because you are the central person in your life. Similarly, the world measures the events of history in reference to Christ's birth date because Jesus is the central person in the world's history. This is true for the skeptic, the agnostic, and the believer alike.

Christ's effect on civilization isn't limited to the B.C. or A.D. initials. Our calendar is the result of his celebrity status, but we can directly attribute other important developments to his influence or individuals. Through the centuries, Christians have been intent on spreading his message of salvation. While there have been abuses to be sure (such as the Crusades, the Inquisition, and charlatan televangelists), major improvements in civilization have accompanied the advancement of the gospel.

There can be no better example than the zeal of Christians in the Middle Ages to make the Bible accessible to common people. Johannes Gutenberg was not desperate to print any romance novel or gossip tabloid. It was the Bible that inspired him to invent a printing press with moveable type. He could have picked something simpler, but the Bible was the first book he printed on his press in 1456. That effort has been recognized as the most significant invention of the second millennium. (Sorry, Bill Gates.)

Christ's message was not solely about a vertical relationship with the heavenly Father; he also emphasized the importance of a horizontal relationship of love and kindness between humans. And so, "in the name of Christ," our civilization was introduced in the Middle Ages to:

- Hospitals to care for the sick and dying;
- Orphanages to protect and care for parentless children;
- Literacy programs intended for all people instead of just the privileged.

And the contributions to civilization in Christ's name have continued through the centuries until now. The problems of our global societies are not best addressed by governments, but by the organized efforts of people who are motivated by Christ's love for the poor and disadvantaged. World Vision, acting in Jesus' name, is the world's largest relief organization, bringing food and supplies to starving people around the globe. And on the local level, faith-based organizations are having the best success with rehabilitation programs for criminals and drug addicts.

There is no doubt about it. Jesus changed the course of civilization, even though he implemented very few of those effects himself. Most were the result of the love and commitment he inspired in others. The accumulative impact of Christ and his followers is such that we cannot conceive of civilization as we know it without his influence. That's why Jesus matters.

Thinking About Why Jesus Matters

- Can you think of any other single person or event that has influenced civilization more than Jesus Christ?

- Do you agree or disagree with the following statement by U.S. President Woodrow Wilson? "Our civilization cannot survive materially unless it be redeemed spiritually."

- Try to imagine what our civilization would look like without the influence of Jesus or his principles. Would it be better or worse? Now consider whether the historical struggles of civilization—and the rise and fall of empires along the way—have been caused by people following the teachings of Jesus too closely, or not enough.

For a child is born to us, a son is given to us. And the government will rest on his shoulders. These will be his royal titles: Wonderful Counselor, Mighty God, Everlasting Father, Prince of Peace. His ever expanding, peaceful government will never end. He will rule forever with fairness and justice from the throne of his ancestor David.

— Isaiah the Prophet[9]

CHAPTER 3
GOVERNMENT

*J*esus would have been a terrible politician. He told people what he thought they *needed* to hear, not what they *wanted* to hear. Although he probably kissed a lot of babies, we can't picture him soliciting campaign contributions at a fancy political fund-raising dinner. And he hung out with the wrong crowd. He spent his time with the poor, the sick, and the unimportant. That is no way to build a power base. Yet Jesus has been more influential in forming governments than any professional politician has been.

Some people expend tremendous effort to remove all traces of Christianity from the government. That is not an easy task.

The United States and many other nations in the Western world have a Christian heritage. It is stamped on their coins, or it may be embedded in the flag salute. In addition, the formational documents of these countries repeatedly refer to God. But even if contemporary references are sanitized to be "Jesus free," history can't be as easily secularized to remove the obvious connection between Christ and the formation of the governments of the world.

Many countries can trace their democratic roots back to the 1600s when the concepts of individual freedom were emerging. The organizational documents of that era stand as a testament to Jesus Christ's influence on the draftsmen and on the people who subscribed to those writings. The Mayflower Compact is a good example. It was the written agreement of Pilgrims who left England to adhere to a Christian form of self-government. The very words of the Compact, often called the "birth certificate" of religious freedom, state that the Pilgrims came to the new land "for the Glory of God, and the Advancement of the Christian Faith."

Other immigrants who left England and Europe to find religious freedom shared similar sentiments in the documentation of their settlements. In 1643, the New England colonies signed a cooperative contract (the "New England Confederation"), which clarified their shared purpose: "We all came into these parts. . .with one and the same end and aim, namely, to advance the Kingdom of our Lord Jesus Christ."

With the breakup of the Soviet Union on December 31, 1991, the art and science of drafting governmental constitutions was revived. These former communist countries used the U. S. Constitution as their primary democratic model. The impact of Jesus on the drafters of the U. S. Constitution cannot be disputed. While references to Christ are not blatant in the Constitution, the reliance on Christian principles by the Founding Fathers is well documented. Regardless of the spin secular historians and jurists have put on the Constitution, the actual American Revolutionary patriots proclaimed the impact of Jesus within those documents. Samuel Adams (Revolutionary War leader, member of the First and Second Continental Congresses, and governor of Massachusetts) said: "These [rights] may be best understood by reading and carefully studying the institutes of the great Law Giver and head of the Christian Church, which are to be found clearly written and promulgated in the New Testament."

Perhaps the best way to realize Jesus' impact on governments is to observe what happens when he is removed from the equation. Such a study reveals that civil liberties are derived from Christian principles and are not forged in atheism or humanism. Any Christian influence was suppressed under Nazi oppression, under Stalin's terror, and under Mao's cultural revolution. These regimes tried to destroy Christianity in their governments. As a result, they slaughtered millions of professing Christians and other innocents. Yet these governments failed in operation and in their ultimate objective.

The teachings and principles of Jesus appear to be the underpinnings of the most successful governments—those that revere freedom and the democratic process.

- Think of governments that have succeeded and those that have failed. What are the common denominators of successful governments? Do the failures have anything in common?

- Many democratic nations employ a strategy of checks and balances among the executive, judicial, and legislative branches of government. It's been said, "If men were angels, no government would be necessary." What is the connection between the doctrine of the separation of powers and the Christian doctrine of the sinfulness of humanity?

- George Washington said, "Mankind, when left to themselves, are unfit for their own government." What does this quote reveal about his attitude toward divine guidance in government operations?

"So if the Son sets you free,
you will indeed be free."

—Jesus[10]

CHAPTER 4

FREEDOM

*R*eligion often gets bogged down in rules and regulations. That's why Jesus rejected institutionalized religion. He was all about freedom. And the ideals he proclaimed two thousand years ago have served as the basis for the privileges that free people enjoy today.

During Christ's time, the Roman Empire was at its peak of world domination. Some of the occupied territories in the Empire were allowed to be somewhat self-governed, as long as the citizens and leaders followed the mandates of the Roman authorities. That's how it was in the regions around Jerusalem where Jesus lived.

Within the parameters of the Roman rule, the Jews were allowed to govern themselves according to the ordinances of their faith. Unfortunately, both levels of bureaucracy were burdensome and abusive. On the secular level, Caesar and his minions imposed oppressive taxes and conscripted people to serve the Empire. At the religious level, the Jewish leaders prescribed a myriad of man-made regulations that had little to do with truly worshiping God, but a lot to do with building the control and power of the temple leaders.

And then Jesus came along. He preached the message of a new Kingdom. Of course, he was talking about the kingdom of God, but many of the people believed he was advocating an overthrow of the Roman government and an overhaul of the temple establishment. In this misunderstood form, Christ's message appealed to multitudes of oppressed people. The elite abhorred his words.

Everyone understood that Jesus was talking about freedom. But in their shortsightedness, they missed the theological nature of his message. Jesus proclaimed that he was the direct connection to God through which people could be freed from their slavery to sin. From Christ's perspective, the eternal effects of sin were to be feared more than the temporal Roman oppression. Likewise, the benefits of spiritual freedom far surpassed the temporary privileges of being a temple official.

Christ's message of freedom didn't die on the cross with him. It survived and his followers promoted it. The apostle

Paul warned against the oppression and judgment that accompany the snare of sin: "So now there is no condemnation for those who belong to Christ Jesus. For the power of the life-giving Spirit has freed you through Christ Jesus from the power of sin that leads to death."[11] But he also emphasized the importance of realizing freedom from the tyranny of misguided religious regulations: "So Christ has really set us free. Now make sure that you stay free, and don't get tied up again in slavery to the law."[12]

The spiritual and religious liberty Jesus Christ proclaimed was the impetus for human freedom and the civil liberties that we enjoy today. In the modern world, countries offering the most freedom are those rooted in Christianity. The Christian concept of freedom from sin and from forced religious conformity leads to a natural desire for civil liberty. The experience of spiritual freedom leads to the desire for personal freedom.

The Christian principles of freedom began in America when the Pilgrims set upon a dangerous excursion to "a new land" to realize a freedom of worship they weren't allowed in the "free" society of England. The spiritual genesis of freedom has been acknowledged throughout the other major events of our country's history:

Regarding the American Revolution, John Quincy Adams noted: "The highest glory of the American Revolution was this: It connected in one indissoluble bond, the principles of civil government with the principles of Christianity."

In the midst of the Civil War, Abraham Lincoln acknowledged: "Those who deny freedom to others deserve it not for themselves, and under a just God, cannot long retain it."

World War II hero General Omar N. Bradley stated: "Freedom—no word was ever spoken that has held out greater hope, demanded greater sacrifice, needed more to be nurtured, blessed more the giver. . .or came closer to being God's will on earth."

The Christ-inspired cause of freedom did not stop in Jerusalem with Jesus' crucifixion in 33 A.D. The principle has thrived despite attempts to extinguish it. And it continues today. . .every time religious or civil liberties are threatened. Whether military action is required to help an oppressed nation gain freedom from a tyrannical dictator or whether a legal action is filed to help a person pursue personal liberty, the concept of freedom stems from Jesus' message.

Thinking About Why Jesus Matters

- Can you think of a country besides the United States in which preserving freedom is so fundamental? What do you believe was the basis for that country's commitment to personal freedom?

- What could the Roman philosopher Seneca have meant when he said: "No man is free who is a slave to the flesh"?

- Notice that the Christ-inspired concepts of freedom that have permeated our culture are not limited to Christians. In what ways have people of other faiths—or those having no religious belief—benefited from the freedoms in our society?

Out of the stump of David's family will grow a shoot—
yes, a new Branch bearing fruit from the old root.
And the Spirit of the LORD will rest on him—
the Spirit of wisdom and understanding,
the Spirit of counsel and might,
the Spirit of knowledge and the fear of the LORD.
He will delight in obeying the LORD.
He will never judge by appearance,
false evidence, or hearsay.
He will defend the poor and the exploited.
He will rule against the wicked and
destroy them with the breath of his mouth.
He will be clothed with fairness and truth.

—ISAIAH THE PROPHET[13]

CHAPTER 5

PROPHECY

What do you think about when you hear the word "prophecy"? Most people automatically relate it to the Great Tribulation, Armageddon, the Second Coming, and all of that end-of-the-world stuff. That's the exciting (and sometimes scary) kind of prophecy the Bible talks about in Revelation.

Most of the prophecies in Revelation have not yet taken place, but plenty of other Bible prophecies have already come true in history. The Bible contains approximately twenty-five hundred prophecies, and about two thousand of them have already been fulfilled. Of these two thousand fulfilled prophecies, nearly three hundred concern the coming Messiah, and Jesus fulfilled all of them when he came to earth.

All of the historical prophecies about Jesus—the ones he has already fulfilled—are recorded in the Old Testament, the part of the Bible recorded before Christ came to earth. These prophecies are scattered throughout the Old Testament, beginning with Genesis, the first book in the Bible, where the first prophecy about Jesus appeared.

> *"From now on, you and the woman will be enemies,*
> *and your offspring and her offspring will be enemies. He*
> *will crush your head, and you will strike his heel."*[14]

God was speaking to Satan (disguised as a snake), and he was talking about Jesus, whom God would someday send to earth to defeat the power of Satan, sin, and death.

The Old Testament prophets did not discuss Jesus by name. Mary, Jesus' mother, gave Jesus his name as she was instructed by the angel Gabriel.[15] The name *Jesus* means "the Lord saves," and this is exactly what the Old Testament prophets predicted. The coming Messiah would be the Deliverer who would come to earth to save God's people.

God was generous and specific in what he told the prophets to write. You could say he left a lot of "clues" so no one would mistake the identity of his Son when he finally came to earth. Here is just a small list of some Old Testament prophecies made hundreds of years before Jesus came to earth:

PROPHECY	FULFILLMENT
He would be born in the town of Bethlehem (Micah 5:2).	Jesus was born in Bethlehem (Luke 2:4–7).
He would be a direct descendent of David, the famous king who killed Goliath and set up his kingdom in Jerusalem (Isaiah 11:1).	Jesus was a descendent of David (Luke 1:31–33).
The Messiah would be born to a virgin (Isaiah 7:14).	Jesus was born of a virgin (Matthew 1:18, 22–23).
Even though he was born in Bethlehem and lived in Nazareth, he would spend his childhood in Egypt (Hosea 11:1).	Jesus was raised in Egypt (Matthew 2:13–21).
The Messiah would have a ceremonial entrance into Jerusalem while riding on a donkey (Zechariah 9:9).	Jesus rode into Jerusalem on a donkey on what we refer to today as Palm Sunday (Matthew 21:2, 4–5).
David predicted the last words of the dying Messiah: "My God, my God! Why have you forsaken me?" (Psalm 22:1).	As he was dying on the cross, Jesus called out, "My God, my God, why have you forsaken me?" (Mark 15:34).

PROPHECY	FULFILLMENT
He would be "counted among those who are sinners" (Isaiah 53:12).	Jesus was crucified with two criminals (Matthew 27:32–35)

———————————

PROPHECY	FULFILLMENT
The Messiah would come back to life after his death (Psalm 16:9–10).	Jesus came back to life after his death (John 20–21).

Just from these eight prophecies about Jesus (and remember, there were three hundred), it would be difficult to deny that Jesus was the Messiah—the long-awaited Savior—the prophets were talking about. Even today, looking at the historical events that took place during Jesus' lifetime, we must be open to the possibility that Jesus was who he said he was: the Son of God sent to save his people from their sins.[16]

Thinking About Why Jesus Matters

- Why is it important that the Bible contains prophecies? What do they show us about God?

- How do the prophecies in the Bible distinguish it from all of the other "holy books" that people read?

- Why was it important that Jesus fulfill the prophecies about himself to the letter? What if any of the prophecies about him had been wrong?

Part Two

Red, brown, yellow, black and white,
All are precious in his sight.
Jesus loves the little children of the world.

—From a children's Sunday school song

Why Jesus Matters in Culture

*E*thnic diversity. Multiculturalism. Cross-cultural. Intercultural. These are some of the current catchwords that reveal an appreciation that our world is expanding. It's not expanding in physical dimensions but in our understanding and appreciation that the earth is populated by people from different cultural groups. We always knew this, of course, but in the past, most of us were not concerned with things that were not pertinent to our own cultural niche.

In past generations, Americans (particularly those of Western European descent) acted like theirs was the culture by which all others should be measured. They felt little compulsion to consider other cultural perspectives. But things are changing. With a new sensitivity, our nation is discovering the rich heritage of our own Native Americans, Mexican-Americans, African-Americans, and Asian-Americans. And we are acquiring an appreciation for cultures that have no "–American" suffix.

Many religions don't translate well across cultures. Each is often specific to the history, philosophies, and traditions of the culture in which it arose. But this is not true with the message of Jesus Christ. His impact transcends cultural lines as easily as it crosses geographic boundaries. Christ's principal teachings don't have to be manipulated to fit into different cultures. They have universal appeal because they have universal application.

Cultural differences aren't limited to ethnicity or nationality. Yes, they include racial distinctions, but they also encompass different economies, philosophies, politics, and fashion. A cultural divide may be gender based or age related. Here again, Christ's teachings are relevant and applicable to all groups.

The apostle Paul revealed the far-reaching application of Christ's teaching. When writing a letter in the first century A.D. to a church in the metropolitan city of Corinth, Paul recognized the diverse cultures represented in that group of believers: "Some of us are Jews, some are Gentiles, some are slaves, and some are free."[17] You don't get much more diverse than that. But he went on to say that those distinctions are never a cause for division when Jesus is the common denominator.

Whatever the cultural context, Jesus matters.

I don't preach a social gospel;
I preach the Gospel, period.
The gospel of our Lord Jesus Christ is
concerned for the whole person.
When people were hungry, Jesus didn't say,
"Now is that political, or social?"
He said, "I'll feed you."
Because the good news to a hungry person is bread.

—BISHOP DESMOND TUTU

Chapter 6

HUMAN RIGHTS

*U*ntil Christ's time, human life had little value in most societies. Certain lives have always been appreciated—people in power have always considered their lives to be precious. But the lives of others—those who were disfavored or who were of little economic worth—were considered of no significance. When Jesus came along, he changed that perspective.

Jesus operated from the premise that every human life has value because all of humanity was created in God's image.[18] He boldly proclaimed that God loved the entire world,[19] and that God was personally interested in every individual.[20] When these Christian concepts work their way into a culture, the result is protection of human rights. Thus, the U. S. Declaration of Independence declares that all people are "created equal" and are "endowed by their Creator with certain inalienable rights."

Proclaiming the value of human life isn't very controversial now, but it was when Jesus preached this message. Certain segments of the population had no political clout and, consequently, were treated as having no value (although the Roman Empire would have collapsed without them). For these despised classes of humanity, Jesus declared the worth of the individual:

Children. In the ancient world, life was cheap, and children were no exception. Child sacrifices were common in the Far East. In the Roman Empire, the decision to have a child was made after it was born. It you wanted it, you kept it; if you didn't want it, you abandoned it at a convenient dumpsite constructed for this purpose. Imagine the paradigm shift when Jesus said: "Let the children come to me. Don't stop them! For the Kingdom of God belongs to such as these."[21]

Women. Before the time of Christ's influence, women in most of the world were viewed on a par with cattle. A wife was her husband's property. Females usually had no dignity or rights. Theirs was a world of servitude, ranking slightly higher than a slave. But Jesus raised the status of women out of societal degradation. In his role as a type of rabbi, he dignified them by letting them study his teachings[22] (which was a privilege reserved for "men only" in the Jewish culture). The apostle Paul reiterated Christ's teaching on the value of a wife. He instructed husbands to love and serve their wives just as Christ loved and served the church.[23] As if using the sacrificial death of Christ as a standard wasn't enough, Paul told the husbands to love their wives as much as those husbands loved themselves. In that male-centered society, this was a major culture shift.

Slaves. Skeptics of Christ often condemn his failure to denounce slavery. Instead, they say, he condoned the evil practice. These critics overlook the fact that Christ actually brought the end of slavery in many cultures. He didn't do it by initiating a mandatory social reform (which would have collapsed the social structure since half of the population of the Roman Empire were slaves). Rather, he worked from the inside out. By re-forming human hearts, over time he reformed the social order. The apostle Paul illustrated Christ's approach by asking a wealthy Christian slave owner to welcome back a runaway slave with kindness and as a beloved brother.[24]

Christ's concepts about the value of life were contrary to the culture of his time. His principles began a cultural shift that has promoted and protected human rights through the centuries. From time to time, as any society moves farther away from Christ's precepts, the value of life in that culture is diminished. If you ever wonder if Jesus matters, just consider if your life matters. It does to him.

THINKING ABOUT WHY GOD MATTERS

- Without Christ's perspective on the value of human life, you might not be alive today.

- Consider a few other cultures or countries where Christianity is not a predominant faith. What are the attitudes in those places towards human rights?

- If Darwin was right and life is merely random happenstance, then "survival of the fittest" is an acceptable ethic. But if Jesus was right and humanity was created in God's image, then the sanctity of life should be our prevailing ethic.

"Do for others what you would
like them to do for you."

—Jesus[25]

CHAPTER 7

BELIEF AND BEHAVIOR

*E*very day our senses are assaulted by the news of horrible things human beings do to one another: shootings, bombings, molestations, murders—the list goes on. Whether such crimes occur in your hometown or across the seas, you can't escape the presence of evil that permeates our world.

It's enough to send the average law abiding citizen into an ironclad bunker—or at the very least into the "safety" of a house armed with the latest in security technology. Yet even the most cautious among us doesn't stay in our self-imposed fortress all the time. Just about every day we venture out to work, shop, visit friends, eat dinner, or see a movie. Even though we may have heard about a carjacking close to home, we don't sell our vehicles and vow to never drive again. We hit the streets and go about our business.

Why do we go out when so many "bad" people fill the world? Because we have faith that most people are pretty much like us—decent, considerate, law-abiding people who trust their fellow human beings to treat them the way they want to be treated. Where does this optimism about the basic decency of human nature come from? From God, of course. He created the human race, and he's the one who allows us to get along with each other.

Even more, God has made it possible for humans to receive and give love, whether we love God or not. We don't have to merely tolerate people. We have the capacity to love them in a way that puts their interests above our own.

If you had to use a word to describe this favor of God on the human race, it would be *grace*. By definition, "grace" means getting something we don't deserve. When God gives us grace, it means he is letting us live in this world in relative peace, getting along with just about everybody.

God's grace gives all people the capacity to live and enjoy this world's benefits. Just for a minute, try to imagine a world without common grace. It wouldn't be a pretty place, and you wouldn't want to live in it. Think of a country ruled by a ruthless dictator where freedom is nonexistent and your life is in constant jeopardy. That's what the entire world would be like without God's grace.

Ultimately God is the *source* of grace, but we have to look to Jesus for the *means* of grace. Remember, grace is something God *gives* to us. What else did God give to us? He gave us Jesus.[26] And it wasn't a spur-of-the-moment decision. God didn't look at the mess the world was in one day and decide, "I think this place and the people in it need to be saved." God knew this long before Jesus came to earth. God knew he would send Jesus long before we knew we needed him.[27]

When Jesus came, he set a new standard for love and decency and goodness that has radiated through the centuries. Jesus didn't just tell us how to live and love, he showed us by his example. He taught his followers to love each other.[28] He said, "Love your neighbor as yourself.[29] And even that's not enough. We are to love our enemies, even those who persecute us.[30]

Not everyone does what Jesus did and taught, but enough people take his words to heart enough of the time to give us a society in which people can get along and help each other. So the next time someone stops to help you when your car breaks down, thank Jesus for making that possible. The next time you feel like giving your neighbor a hand, remember that Jesus is the reason. That's why Jesus matters to you and the world.

Thinking About Why Jesus Matters

- Can you think of a time when Jesus loved his enemies?

- Can you think of a time when you loved your enemies?

- Isn't it amazing how Jesus positively impacts people, even those who don't take him seriously?

"Wherever your treasure is,
there your heart and thoughts will also be."

—J ESUS [31]

CHAPTER 8

MONEY

*A*sk the average person what Jesus thought about money, and he or she will probably say he hated it. After all, he lived simply, he owned nothing except the clothes on his back, and one time Jesus got so angry with the money-changers in the temple that he went after them with a whip.

When Jesus talked about money, he seemed to discourage people from getting too much of it. On different occasions Jesus said, "You cannot serve both God and money"[32] and "How hard it is for rich people to get into the kingdom of God."[33]

Why did Jesus seem so antagonistic toward money? Are Christ's followers supposed to pursue the simple life rather than accumulate wealth? This is the understanding many people have: If you want to be a Christian, forget about being rich; and if you want to be rich, forget about being a Christian.

This may be what people believe about Jesus and money, but it's not accurate. Rather than discouraging us from being productive and making money, Jesus consistently taught the value of using money for good. Rather than declaring that money is evil, Jesus taught that a person's attitude toward money is the issue, not money itself.

Jesus once told a story of three servants who were given sums of money to invest for their master.[34] Each servant was given a different amount of money according to his abilities. The first servant, who was given the most money, invested his portion and doubled it. The second servant, who received a lesser amount, also doubled his money. The third servant, who received the least amount, buried the money for safekeeping. Then the master asked for an accounting of the resources he had given his servants. The first two explained how they had doubled their money. Their master praised them for being faithful with what he had given them. But things didn't go so well for the third servant. When the master learned that he had buried the money, he took it away from him and gave it to the first servant, declaring, "To those who use well what they are given, even more will be given, and they will have an abundance. But from those who are unfaithful, even what little they have will be taken away."

The lessons from this story, in which God is the master and we are the servants, speak volumes about the way Jesus viewed money, possessions, and productivity. Some religions deny the importance of the material world. By contrast, Christianity—based on Christ's life and teaching—claims that the material world is very important.

In fact, there is clear evidence that the world is a much better place materially and economically because of Jesus and his teachings. We have already heard from Jesus in the area of productivity. Beyond that, the Bible teaches the need for us to work. Far from being a curse, work is a mandate from God. Labor, and the money we receive for our labor, provides the means for us to care for our families and ourselves. Work also enables us to care for others' needs—especially those who can't work and be productive.

Since Jesus walked the earth (working as a carpenter, by the way), the world has been more productive and prosperous. Thanks to the work ethic of Christians, most people's standard of living has gotten better, not worse. And just what is the Christian work ethic? There are several characteristics:

- We are not to worry about money, because our heavenly Father knows what we need. He will give us all we need if we make him number one in our lives.[35]
- We are not to steal or covet others' property.[36]
- God has promised to give us the wisdom and strength to do our daily tasks.[37]
- Those who work wisely will be rewarded.[38]
- In everything we do and in all we produce, we are to thank God and honor him.[39]
- We are responsible to share with those in need.[40]

Contrast this philosophy of work and productivity, which has served as the basis of capitalism and the free enterprise system for nearly two thousand years, with other economic systems that discourage productivity and suppress the God-given abilities of working people.

Of course, with productivity and prosperity comes great responsibility. It isn't enough to simply make money for personal gain. As Jesus once said, "Much is required from those to whom much is given."[41] Jesus knows the human heart better than anyone. He knows how the love of money can lead to greed and indifference to others' needs. He knows that money can become a barrier between God and us.

Money can become a source of pride over our abilities and successes. That's why Jesus taught that we cannot serve both God and money. We must put God and his priorities first. The best way to do this is to understand that the stuff we have and the money we make are on loan from God. He made them and he owns them. Our job is to be good stewards of what God has allowed us to have. That means being productive, and it also means being generous.

Jesus taught that rather than accumulating wealth here on earth, we should store our treasure in heaven by giving to those in need. As much as possible, we need to invest our money in people and programs that have eternal value—rather than just temporary gain.[42]

Thinking About Why Jesus Matters

- How does knowing that Jesus is interested in your money change the way you make and spend the money you have?

- Because everything we have comes from God, we can't give him anything that doesn't already belong to him.

- It isn't how rich or poor we are that matters, but what we do with what God has given us.

Jesus is not a blue-eyed right-winger,
as some have implied;
nor is he a guilt-ridden liberal or compromising centrist.
Jesus is the one who entered the world
among the dispossessed and the outcasts
to announce an entirely new way of thinking and living.
The way of Jesus and the prophets
isn't just a welfare program;
it calls for a change of heart,
a revolution of the spirit,
a transformation of our consciousness.

—Jim Wallis

CHAPTER 9

POLITICS

*T*here was a time when Jesus was politically correct. People claimed he was on their side when they wanted to prove they were right about a controversial issue. Of course, that was a while ago. . .before anyone even knew about political correctness.

Not so gradually, over the last two decades or so, Jesus has become politically *incorrect*. You can squeak by and include a reference to "God" into social discourse (because a veiled mention of "God" could be a reference to the god of any number of religions). A nondescript god is acceptable because it fits in society's tolerance of religious pluralism—a belief that all religions are basically the same with little distinguishable significance. But

"Jesus" is a political taboo. To align yourself with him is to risk wearing the label as someone who is intolerant of others.

The word of the day in politics seems to be tolerance. Accordingly, political strategies are designed to advance a party's appearance of tolerance. So, if Jesus is equated with intolerance, then it is understandable that the major political parties don't seek his endorsement of their candidates.

But why is Jesus getting a bad rap for being intolerant? Perhaps because Christ claimed: "I am the way, the truth, and the life. No one can come to the Father except through me."[43] A single way to God does imply exclusivity, but an exclusive pathway doesn't mean that the thoroughfare is restricted. All religions are based on a claim that their belief system is the only true one. (Does a devout Muslim really believe that a Buddhist's faith is true? Can a committed Orthodox Jew believe that a Catholic's belief is true?) By their very nature, each faith system holds to the belief that it exclusively possesses ultimate truth.

Actually, Jesus set a noble standard that political parties should follow. While he spoke of truth, he didn't limit his message to a select few. He wasn't interested in an elitist following; he made his teachings relevant and broad enough to include everyone. "For God so loved *the world*,"[44] he said. His invitation was wide open: "Come to me, all of you who are weary and carry heavy burdens, and I will give you rest."[45]

Whether he is politically correct or not, Jesus' impact on contemporary politics is best demonstrated by the fact that he might simultaneously support certain planks in the platform of opposing political parties. From his teachings, we are inspired to:

- Care for the poor;
- Use our wealth to benefit others who need it; and
- Support the government's tax programs.

Yet, in almost apparent contrast, his teachings also encourage:

- The practice of personal responsibility;
- Disciplined money management and self-reliance for one's self and family; and
- An understanding that society's problems are not ultimately solved through bureaucratic methods.

Although his teachings appear to have contradictory political perspectives, that is only because we live in a society with polarized political agendas. When you examine Christ's teachings apart from the political analysis, you can see he offered a simplified yet effective method for social governance and interaction: "Love your neighbor as yourself."[46] Wouldn't that be a great campaign slogan for any political party? Of course, since everyone has a different personal agenda, we probably couldn't agree on what that slogan means in practice.

Perhaps it is a good thing that Jesus wasn't a politician. His message was too simple for the cutthroat world of politics.

THINKING ABOUT WHY JESUS MATTERS

- What teachings of Jesus would appeal to the Republican Party? Which of his teachings would appeal to the Democrats?

- If Jesus were alive today, which political party would he join?

- What aspects about Jesus would make him an unattractive candidate for political office? Would anything about him appeal to the voters?

After Jesus finished speaking,
the crowds were amazed at his teaching,
for he taught as one who had real authority—
quite unlike the teachers of religious law.

—St. Matthew[47]

CHAPTER 10

EDUCATION

*J*esus was the greatest teacher who ever lived. As he walked the earth interacting with people, he didn't discuss trivial things. Jesus taught others about the right way to live and the way to please God. Whether he was having a one-on-one conversation or addressing a massive crowd, Jesus was the Master Teacher.

When religious leaders came to Jesus for advice, they called him *Teacher*.[48] After Jesus delivered his famous "Sermon on the Mount," the crowds were amazed at his teaching, for he taught as one who had real authority.[49] Just because Jesus had real authority doesn't mean he was like a gruff, heartless professor who enjoys confounding students. Jesus taught in a way ordinary people could understand. He used words and told stories that illustrated the truth he taught. The Bible says, "The common people heard him gladly."[50]

It wasn't just the common people who were drawn to Jesus. Children loved him, too. One time his own disciples tried to keep some kids from "bothering" Jesus, but he said, "Let the children come to me. Don't stop them! For the Kingdom of heaven belongs to such as these."[51]

Everything Jesus taught revolved around the truth: the truth about the world, the truth about relationships, and the truth about God. The things he taught and the way he taught them set the example for all great teachers who came after him. And it wasn't just teachers who followed Jesus' pattern. Many of the great schools and universities established after Jesus lived have been founded on his teachings and teaching methods.

For example, Harvard University, America's oldest and most prestigious institution of higher learning, was founded in 1636, just sixteen years after the Pilgrims landed on Plymouth Rock. What many people don't know is that this venerable university was established on the religious beliefs of the Puritans, who came to America to openly practice their faith in Jesus. The official seal of Harvard University proclaims *Veritas*, the Latin word for *Truth*. And what is truth? Jesus said it best: "I am the way, the truth, and the life."[52]

That Harvard was founded on Christian principles was not

unusual. Hundreds of colleges and universities were established by Christians who wanted to teach young people the truth about every aspect of the universe. Christians, motivated by the pattern of teaching and the thirst for knowledge set forth in the Bible and exemplified by Jesus, were pioneers and promoters of education around the world. They understood that education is incomplete unless the intellect is united with the heart and the heart united with God.

No one understood this more than Jesus. Once Jesus went to the temple to teach. The religious leaders were astonished that Jesus knew so much, because as far as they were concerned, he had not studied at their schools. "How does he know so much?" they asked. Jesus responded by saying, "I'm not teaching my own ideas, but those of God who sent me."[53]

Even Jesus, the Son of God, equal to God in every way, knew that all truth comes from God. He went on to say that those who present their own ideas—ideas that are not rooted in God and his truth—are merely trying to bring attention to themselves and their accomplishments rather than to God and all he has done.

You can get all the education in the world, but unless the things you learn point to God, you won't have the complete picture. Jesus taught this and practiced it, setting an example for everyone who followed him.

- Very few colleges and universities founded on biblical principles and the teachings of Jesus have stayed true to their beginnings. What has been the result of this "falling away"?

- Is it possible to get a well-rounded, objective education at a college or university that suppresses or denies the truth about God and the teachings of Jesus? What would you have to do?

- Ultimately all truth is God's truth. Therefore, the most important thing you can do in the course of your education is to pursue the truth.

PART THREE

It is extremely hard for a Christian
to look straight at his religion
without regarding science out of the corner of his eye,
or to face science
without a similar side-glance at religion.

—GEORGE TYRRELL

WHY JESUS MATTERS IN SCIENCE

As people living in the twenty-first century, we pride ourselves in our scientific accomplishments. We can hardly remember a time when we didn't have space travel, computers, and a cure for the common cold (oops, we haven't come up with that one yet). Our technology is so impressive that we can hardly imagine what it was like to live without electricity, running water, and cell phones.

When we think of Jesus and the time he lived on the earth, we tend to imagine that he couldn't possibly relate to our technologically advanced world. We picture him in sandals, drawing pictures in the dirt. We think his teachings apply to our moral and spiritual lives but that when it comes to scientific knowledge, we're pretty much on our own. We conclude that people who don't follow Christ are just as likely to make discoveries as those who do. Maybe more likely.

What a mistake we make when we separate Jesus from the universe he created. The Bible claims that Jesus, who was born in a barn and never ventured more than a few hundred miles from his hometown, is the Creator of the universe.[54] As the Creator, don't you think Jesus would know everything there is to know about how the universe operates? And if he knows everything about the universe now, is it possible that Jesus knew about it when he walked the earth?

Just look how he rearranged atoms and molecules when he turned the water into wine.[55] He knew how the atmosphere works. Just see how he exerted authority over the wind and the sea.[56] Jesus knew everything about the human body. Just look how he raised a dead man back to life.[57]

How can you separate the creation from the Creator? When you think about it this way, there's nothing we can know about the universe that Jesus doesn't already know. There's nothing we can discover and no technological barrier we can cross without seeing Jesus on the other side. Rather than leaving Jesus in the first century, we need to bring him into the twenty-first century and thank him for every good and beneficial advancement and discovery he enables humans to make.

Every glimpse of God is his gift,
to lead us to long more for that most blessed,
ever-longing, ever satisfying knowledge of him,
which will be the bliss of eternity.

—EDWARD PUSEY

CHAPTER II

KNOWLEDGE

The Bible says Jesus came to earth for one purpose: to find and to save those who are separated from God.[58] He came as a light to a world bathed in darkness.[59] The Bible says Jesus gave light to everyone, even those who did not receive him.[60]

What does this mean? Very simply, yet very profoundly, it means that all people are enlightened in their understanding of what is true. They may not always follow what they know is true, especially concerning the things of God, but they know the difference between right and wrong.[61] The reason we are "enlightened" in the first place is because Jesus brought his light to us.

This enlightenment isn't restricted to the moral realm.

Because Jesus exists, we have the ability to know and to understand how the world works. This knowledge and understanding have always been present in the human race, but after Jesus came into our physical universe and lived among us, knowledge accelerated. Even the most vocal critics of Christianity acknowledge that we can attribute the development of modern science to the Christian worldview.

Why? Because Christianity is based on the teachings and the life of Christ, who taught the truth about how the world works. He taught that God is a rational, knowable, personal Being who desires to have a relationship with us. God created us to enjoy and interact with the physical world, which operates according to natural, predictable laws (also created by God).

Contrast this to human philosophies and other religions, which generally believe one of two things: that the spiritual and the physical worlds are not connected; or that the two have no distinction. For example, the Greek philosophers before Christ did not believe the physical world could be changed. You could think about the world and come to certain conclusions, but you could never interact with it in a way that would improve your life. In our time, some religions and belief systems teach that the material world is evil. Not only can we not change the world, but we must also avoid getting too involved in the world. At best, we need to separate ourselves from it.

Christianity stands alone as a religion that believes there is a knowable, rational, personal God who is the Creator of the world and the Source of all truth. Because he is knowable and rational, the world he created is also knowable and rational. It operates according to natural, knowable, predictable laws. If it didn't, there would be no basis for knowledge.

In his graciousness and love, God has allowed us to discover and to know the "secrets" of the universe. In fact, he has commanded us to do so! Immediately after he finished creating the universe, God instructed the human race:

> *"Multiply and fill the earth and subdue it. Be masters over the fish and birds and all the animals."* [62]

This didn't mean that the earth and everything in it were to become our slaves. God expects us to take care of his creation. To do that, we have to *know* everything we can about the universe. In a very real sense, God wants us to *master* what our world is all about and give him the credit and the glory for the incredible things we learn.

You see, God hasn't given us the ability to grasp the truth about the universe and how it works just so we can pat ourselves on the back and say, "Look how much we know." The worst thing that can happen is for clever humans to proclaim, "We don't need God. We know everything we need to know!" That kind of arrogant knowledge separates us from God.

God has given us the ability to know how the universe works so we will turn our hearts to him. And through Jesus, he has given us the ability to know God and to understand how he works. That's what true knowledge is all about, and that's why Jesus matters.

THINKING ABOUT WHY JESUS MATTERS

- Are there things about the universe that are "unknowable"? Give some examples.

- Are there things about God that are "unknowable"? Give some examples. What are some things you know about God? How does that affect the way you live?

- It isn't what you know that counts, but what you do with what you know.

"For God so loved the world that he gave his only Son,
so that everyone who believes in him
will not perish but have eternal life."

—Jesus[63]

CHAPTER 12

EXPLORATION AND DISCOVERY

*P*eople are naturally curious. They aren't content to leave things the way they are. They want to know how things work, and they won't settle for staying in their own neighborhoods. They want to see what lies on the other side of the mountain or across the sea.

Where did this desire to discover come from? Why is humankind so determined to investigate every square inch of the earth and the universe? We can point to our Creator, who has blessed each of us with two things: the ability to distinguish truth from error, which comes in very handy when you are conducting science experiments or navigating uncharted waters; and the restless desire to improve and make a better life for ourselves.

If we weren't endowed with the ability to think, reason, and explore, we would never venture beyond our own backyards or do everything we could to improve our lives. But a restlessness was put in the human heart by our Creator. We want to explore new frontiers, whether on land, in the sea, or in space. We want to discover new ways of doing things, invent amazing devices, and develop the earth's natural resources for everyone's benefit.

Part of this desire to improve our location and our lot in life probably comes from the desire in all of us for something more and better. The old spiritual song that begins "This world is not my home, I'm just a passin' through" gets to the crux of the matter very simply. As good as things are here on earth, there is a sense in every person that this is not as good as it gets. All it takes is a violent storm or a life-threatening illness, and we suddenly realize the world can be cruel. So we dream of a sunnier climate or a life free from disease and pain.

Or sometimes we are perfectly happy where we are, but the desire for change comes anyway. So it was with Abram, later to become Abraham, the great patriarch who is the earthly father of the world's three monotheistic religions (Judaism, Christianity, and Islam). Abram was a wealthy man who had no plans to leave his birthplace. Then God told him to abandon his country, his relatives, and the family home for a new place where God would use him in incredible ways.[64]

Or how about Moses, the great deliverer of Israel? He was minding his own business when God told him to go to Egypt to help God's people find a new home flowing with milk and honey, where the cruel hand of their oppressor would not follow them.[65]

Then there was Jesus, who left his heavenly home and gave up his rights as God so he could come to earth as a human. Talk about an adventurous journey! God became human so he could experience all of our frailties and suffering and eventually our death.

We might be able to identify with the earthbound journeys of Abraham and Moses, but we can only imagine the level of love and commitment that led Jesus to embark on his great cosmic adventure on our behalf. In our lifetimes, most of us will feel the frailties and taste the suffering that go with being human, but not to the extent that Jesus did. For at the end of his sojourn, he paid the ultimate price so we could ultimately go to a place where no frailty or suffering or death exists.

Once Jesus was talking with his disciples about the difficulties he would face. He even predicted that one of his followers would betray him. "Don't be troubled," Jesus assured them. "You trust God, now trust in me. There are many rooms in my Father's home, and I am going to prepare a place for you. If this were not so, I would tell you plainly. When everything is ready, I will come and get you, so that you will always be with me where I am. And you know where I am going and how to get there."[66]

That is the ultimate extreme adventure, the final destination, the perfect resting place we all long for. It's the place the Bible calls heaven, where time stops and eternity begins. All of our desires for a better place and a better life on earth are good. God has given us the gift of exploration and discovery. But all of our adventures and achievements will pale in comparison to that great day when we go to the place Jesus has prepared.

THINKING ABOUT WHY JESUS MATTERS

- What do you think is the greatest human achievement in the history of the world?

- Great discoveries always improve the lives of others.

- The greatest adventure anyone can experience is to explore God and discover Jesus.

A vast crowd brought him the lame, blind, crippled,
mute, and many others with physical difficulties,
and they laid them before Jesus.
And he healed them all. The crowd was amazed!
Those who hadn't been able to speak were talking,
the crippled were made well,
the lame were walking around,
and those who had been blind could see again!

— ST. MATTHEW[67]

CHAPTER 13

HEALTH AND MEDICINE

*H*ealth care during Jesus' time was primitive. Hospitals did not exist, so banish any notion of a sterile operating room! There was no anesthesia, so when a patient "was put to sleep" in those days, it was either permanently or because the intense pain sent the patient into shock. Disease was rampant. Deformities prevailed. The average life expectancy was twenty-eight years due to the high fatality rate for anyone who became sick.

Anyone with an illness or an infirmity at the time of Christ was more likely to die than be cured. So, it's no wonder that Jesus became known as the "Great Physician." The Gospel accounts are filled with stories of Jesus healing the sick. And apparently, in contrast to modern medicine, he didn't specialize. The biblical references report his healing of the blind, the lame, the mute, the bleeding, and the crazy. There are even descriptions of his raising the dead back to life.

Some skepticism exists about the legitimacy of Christ's healing miracles, but we don't need to debate the authenticity of medical miracles to acknowledge Christ's impact on medical science. Whether or not healing miracles actually happened is irrelevant to the fact that Jesus has been the greatest influence on the progress of health care through the last twenty centuries. His universal influence isn't due to individual miracles (which would be important to the person who experienced it, but of little global impact). Rather, Jesus matters in the realm of health and medicine because he inspired compassion in people to attend to the sick and dying. The love of Christ, not the cures of Christ, has prompted scientists, physicians, nurses, and missionaries to bring medical help to people around the globe.

Jesus has been the inspiration and motivation for some of health care's greatest advancements in the last two thousand years:

Hospitals. Under the auspices of the Christian church (through the Council of Nicaea), the first organized establishment of hospitals began in 325 A.D. In the United States, the forerunners of hospitals were "almshouses" started by Quakers. The leading historian on the creation of hospitals in America is Professor Charles E. Rosenberg of the University of Pennsylvania, who has said early hospitals in the U. S. were "framed and motivated by the responsibilities of Christian stewardship."

Nursing Organizations. The predecessors of modern nurses were women who joined convents specifically to attend to the sick and dying. Florence Nightingale, the founder of modern nursing was a devout Christian woman. She began her work in a Christian commune in Germany. She distinguished herself by aiding wounded soldiers in the Crimean War, and she established the first school for nurses in London. Florence Nightingale often said that Christ had called her into his service.

The Red Cross. Henry Dunant, a Swiss banker and philanthropist, was internationally known for establishing the Young Men's Christian Association (YMCA) in Geneva in the 1850s. When he witnessed the horror of death and injury on the battlefields of the Napoleonic wars, he founded the International Red Cross as a cooperative effort of nations to render "neutral" medical assistance. This was clearly a Christian effort, and that intent was reflected by the symbol of the red cross. Muslims recognized the influence of Jesus on the organization, so when Turkey joined in 1876 (as the first

Muslim nation), it changed the symbol and name in its country to the Red Crescent.

Medical Research. Louis Pasteur is recognized as one of the greatest biologists of all time. At first his research was controversial because he opposed the Darwinian notion of spontaneous generation. His scientific proof, however, persuaded the medical establishment to change its manner of treating disease. Pasteur's Christian faith did not allow him to accept a notion of the naturalistic origin of life. His biographer, Rene Vallery-Radot, wrote that Pasteur's belief in Christ pervaded Pasteur's whole life and his worldview.

Global Advancements. The presence of modern medical facilities in third world countries is a result of Jesus' influence. Because of their commitment to Christ, missionary organizations have constructed thousands of hospitals all over the world. In many parts of the world, Christian organizations were the first to help lepers, the blind, the deaf, and the crippled.

Jesus probably made actual, physical contact with a few thousand people who were sick or injured. But the number of people who have been aided in his name during the past two thousand years is incalculable.

Thinking About Why Jesus Matters

- Do you know of someone who has been inspired by Christ to devote time to some sort of humanitarian service? How do you think faith in Jesus can stimulate such devoted service?

- Can you name an international organization that offers medical assistance in the name of Christ? Were any hospitals in your area established by Christian organizations?

- Would you rather: (a) Cure several hundred people of a terrible disease; or (b) Inspire millions of people to bring medical assistance to those who need it around the world for centuries after your death?

"Therefore, go and make disciples of all the nations,
baptizing them in the name of
the Father and the Son and the Holy Spirit."

—JESUS[68]

CHAPTER 14

TECHNOLOGY

*J*esus was not a gadget guy. Admittedly, he lived two thousand years ago, when there wasn't a True Value hardware store in every neighborhood and men weren't eagerly awaiting delivery of the next Sharper Image catalog. But the society in which he lived wasn't totally primitive, either. In parts of the Roman Empire, people had mastered the complexities of indoor plumbing and forced-air ventilation.

Jesus, however, didn't appear to be concerned with technological advancements of his day. Oh, sure, he probably helped out as a kid in his father's carpentry shop. So maybe he had a familiarity with basic hand tools. But he must not have had any fascination with them. As an adult, all evidence points to his living the simplest of existences. He had a cloak and his sandals, and that was about it.

Jesus wasn't opposed to industrial innovation; he just wasn't interested in it. He had bigger things on his mind. . .like spreading his gospel message. He wanted to get his message to the people, and he wanted his followers to do the same thing in his absence. And this is where we begin to see Christ's impact on emerging technologies. Not that he invented or used technology, but the followers of Christ have always implemented developmental technologies in their efforts to spread the gospel.

Since the first century A.D., Christians have been impassioned in their efforts to take Christ's message to others. Christians consider themselves to have been given a "Great Commission" by Christ to take his message to "all the nations."[69] And this task and privilege isn't limited to geopolitical boundaries. The charge for spreading the gospel message extends "to the ends of the earth."[70] You can't go any farther than that.

In their effort to take the message of Christ to everyone everywhere, Christians have always been pioneers in emerging technologies:

Printing Press. Gutenberg's printing press with moveable type doesn't sound "high tech" today, but in 1456 it was an ultramodern advancement. Christians wasted no time in putting this innovation to work in their evangelistic efforts. As a matter of fact, the Holy Bible was the first book Gutenberg put into mass production with his newfangled invention.

Radio and Television Broadcasting. Guglielmo Marconi made the first long-wave radio signal broadcast in 1901, but radio broadcasting didn't become widespread until the 1920s. Christians were there as it happened, with the first Christian broadcast in 1921 on radio station KDKA in Pittsburgh. Because radio knew no walls or fences, for decades mission organizations preferred this media to reach people trapped in countries where preaching the gospel was not allowed. The development of television was the same, with Christian organizations involved in the earliest stages. And Christians are at the cutting edge of recent technological advancements in satellite broadcasting. Currently, the state of the art in satellite broadcasting finds only three high-power direct broadcast satellite (DBS) companies operating in the United States today; one of them is owned and licensed by a Christian organization (with a stated purpose of providing TV and radio channels that espouse Christian values and communicate the gospel of Jesus Christ). Encompassing all media formats that use the airwaves, the National Religious Broadcasters (NRB) is an international association of Christian communicators with more than seventeen hundred member organizations representing millions of viewers, listeners, and readers.

The Internet. And let's not forget the World Wide Web. Sites devoted to Christian doctrine have existed from the outset. A quick word search for "Jesus" at www.google.com will list 16,500,000 sites.

Some Christian activity that advanced technology was profit driven, but most of the innovations developed and refined by Christian organizations had no profit motive. These efforts were prompted by a desire to fulfill that "Great Commission" of taking the message of Christ to people of all nations.

THINKING ABOUT WHY JESUS MATTERS

- If you had a message you believed could change lives for the better, how would you get that message to as many people as possible?

- Consider the types of organizations which might be interested in providing technology to impoverished third world countries. There are manufacturers (looking to sell products), broadcasters (looking for advertising revenues), and mission agencies (looking to spread their message). Who has the strongest motivation?

- You can easily download the entire Bible onto your PDA. How many other books would you estimate are available in a similar way? What does your answer tell you about the universally recognized importance of making the Bible available on developing technologies?

Because of the miraculous signs
he did in Jerusalem at the Passover celebration,
many people were convinced that
he was indeed the Messiah.

—ST. JOHN[71]

CHAPTER 15

MIRACLES

*T*here is no doubt about it. Jesus is controversial. He was two thousand years ago, and he still is today (perhaps even more than ever).

Two factors combine to make Jesus so controversial. First: He claimed to be God.[72] However, any lunatic can claim to be God (and many have); but every wacko with a god-complex doesn't achieve the notoriety of Christ. So it isn't just the *claim* to be God that sets Jesus apart. Now we come to the second factor that contributes to the Christ controversy. With Christ there was something that gave his claims of divinity apparent credibility—he performed miracles. (A bit of the supernatural is pretty good evidence if someone is questioning your divinity credentials.)

For a moment, let's set aside Christ's claim to be God and focus on his ability to perform miracles. Did they really occur, or were the reports of Christ's supernatural activities exaggerations by his enthusiastic biographers? From a historical perspective, there is ample evidence to conclude that those seemingly miraculous events actually occurred. Historians have certain standards for determining the reliability of ancient accounts. Jesus' miracles pass these critical tests.

For example: There were eyewitness accounts of the miracles; these reports were recorded in writing early after the miracles occurred (as opposed to being preserved through generations by oral tradition); multiple sources attested to the miracles; and adversaries of Jesus and agnostic witnesses admitted that the miracles occurred. By any objective standard of scholarship, the historicity of the occurrence of the miracles must be accepted.

Of course, accepting the appearance of miraculous events doesn't mean they were truly supernatural. If we accept that something unexplainable happened, then we must determine if the cause was supernatural or sleight of hand. Obviously, not everything that is incomprehensible to the observer is supernatural. Illusionists like David Copperfield and David Blaine mystify audiences with accomplishments that seem inexplicable, but no one wonders if a supernatural influence is involved (and these tricks suddenly seem mundane when you watch TV's "Secrets of the Master Magicians Revealed").

The state of science at Christ's time was rudimentary compared with modern scientific knowledge. So skeptics of the miracles in A.D. 33 might have thought, "Those miracles are a load of bunk. But you have to hand it to that Jesus. He is a grand illusionist. We can't understand it now, but just wait. In another decade or so, someone will figure out how he did it."

Well, more than a decade has passed. In fact, science has had approximately two thousand years to figure out how Jesus "did it." Yet there is still no reasonable explanation for those occurrences other than supernatural intervention.

So the mystery still remains. Were those apparent miracles real or fraudulent?

Since the miracles have not been debunked, we must still wonder about the first question: whether Jesus was God as he claimed to be.

And so the controversy continues.

- What do you think philosopher Blaise Pascal meant when he said: "Had it not been for the miracles, there would have been no sin in not believing in Jesus Christ."

- Is it necessary to believe the credibility of the miracles in order to believe Christ's claim that he was God?

- Imagine that someone were to find a nonsupernatural explanation for Jesus' miracles. Conversely, imagine that the scientific community were to issue a unanimous finding that the miracles have no explanation besides a divine source. In either case, would the controversy surrounding Christ cease?

PART FOUR

The fine arts once divorcing themselves from truth
are quite certain to fall mad,
if they do not die.

—THOMAS CARLYLE

WHY JESUS MATTERS IN THE ARTS

*V*ery often when we refer to people who have a talent for writing or painting or music or design, we say they have a "gift." That's not to say that great or even good literature just happens, or that a beautiful composition comes with no effort. Even the most talented artists, musicians, and architects must study their particular craft and work hard to produce truly beautiful things.

On the other hand, great effort alone doesn't necessarily produce objects of beauty. The gift or talent must be there for the effort to result in something everyone can agree is beautiful. Where does this gift come from? Well, have you ever heard the expressions "God-given talent" or "a gift from God"? When we recognize extraordinary abilities in the arts, we don't say, "He picked up that talent in his travels" or "She was a terrible artist before she enrolled in that art class, but now she's got a painting hanging in the Metropolitan Museum."

Does a talent for the arts really come from God? If so, why don't all of us have such a gift? The truth is, God has given every person the gift of art. Now, we may not all have the ability to produce artistic things, but we all have the ability—or at least the capacity—to appreciate them. That's the gift God has given each of us, and it's a gift made possible by Jesus.

You see, beautiful art—whether expressed in a painting, a sculpture, a poem, or a song—is most effective when it accurately reflects the beauty of God's creation. This includes the timeless nature of the human spirit as well as the vast panorama of nature. The Bible says that everything in this world has been made by God through Jesus, and that Jesus holds all creation together.[73]

In this section on the arts, we're going to see how the beauty and the wonder of our world and the people in it are here because of Jesus. Without Jesus, the harmony and beauty we see in nature and in the human heart would not exist.

Fix your thoughts on what is
true and honorable and right.
Think about things that are
pure and lovely and admirable.
Think about things that are
excellent and worthy of praise.

—Paul the Apostle[74]

CHAPTER 16

ART

There's an old saying: "Beauty is in the eye of the beholder." This implies that what one person finds ugly is beautiful to another. Now, this may be true when you're talking about someone you love or an old house you're fixing up or a drawing scribbled by your three-year-old child. But you can't really apply such subjectivity to the beauty we find in God's creation, usually referred to as "nature."

No rational, thinking person would look at a garbage dump and remark, "Now that's a pretty sight" (unless he happened to own the garbage dump). Likewise, a crowd of people on a Hawaiian beach looking at a magnificent sunset will not have differing opinions on the majesty of the moment. When something is beautiful in nature—whether it's a sunset, a full-bloomed flower, or one of God's creatures—we all recognize it.

That's because the same God who created the universe in all of its beauty and harmony and order also created us. In Genesis we read that after he finished his work of creation—including creating people in his image—"God looked over all he had made, and he saw it was excellent in every way."[75] He recognized the beauty of what he had created. As God's image bearers, we also have the ability to appreciate this created harmony and beauty, because God built these same qualities into us.

So what does all of this have to do with art? At its best, great art portrays great beauty, the kind of beauty we all recognize. Great art communicates order rather than chaos. It brings peace, not turmoil, to your soul. That's not to say that the only beautiful art is that which accurately represents Hawaiian sunsets or floral arrangements. But the kind of art we all recognize as lovely should somehow reflect the truth and goodness and beauty of God. Or it should remind us how futile it is to live apart from God.

When the apostle Paul encouraged the church in Philippi to "think about things that are excellent and worthy of praise," he wasn't just referring to things that are true and virtuous. He was also implying that we are to think about Jesus, the source of truth and virtue. In another letter to the church at Colosse, Paul wrote that Jesus is also the source of all creation, and he is the one who holds everything together.[76] What does that mean, and what does it have to do with art and beauty? It's very simple, but very profound.

Not long after God finished his work of creation and declared it excellent, sin entered the world. Theologians call it the Fall. The implications of the Fall were huge. Not only was humankind separated from God, but nature itself was crushed and broken.[77] Yet it could have been a lot worse. God could have destroyed his creation because of sin. But he didn't. Instead, God sent Jesus to make things right, both in the human heart and in nature. When the Bible says that Jesus "holds all creation together," you can take that literally. Because of Jesus, we have beauty and harmony. Because of Jesus, we have art.

The word "art" comes from a word meaning "to fit together." It's the same word found in the word "artisan," describing someone who fits together useful objects of beauty. That's what Jesus does for broken people in a broken world. He takes the broken pieces and fits them together into something that is beautiful and useful.

In his brilliant Bible paraphrase *The Message*, Eugene Peterson says it this way:

> *He was supreme in the beginning and—leading the resurrection parade—he is supreme in the end. From beginning to end he's there, towering far above everything, everyone. So spacious is he, so roomy, that everything of God finds its proper place in him without crowding. Not only that, but all*

the broken and dislocated pieces of the universe—people and things, animals and atoms—get properly fixed and fit together in vibrant harmonies, all because of his death, his blood that poured down from the Cross.[78]

THINKING ABOUT WHY JESUS MATTERS

- How would you defend this statement in an art class: "Because of Jesus, we have art"?

- What happens when we don't think about things that are true and honorable and pure and lovely?

- When art fails to connect with God in some way, it fails to connect with people in any way.

Had Jesus never been born,
music would sound very different
from what we're used to. . . .
Music today would probably sound
somewhat similar to what we hear
in the Middle East or Far East.
There never would have developed
the cantata, the concerto, or the symphony.

—D. James Kennedy

CHAPTER 17

MUSIC

*I*n the opinion of many musical scholars, the greatest composer who ever lived was Johann Sebastian Bach (1685–1750). He developed and refined music theory that remains the cornerstone for modern melodies. Many of the great contemporary rock, country, and pop recording artists developed their instrumental skills playing Bach compositions. There seems to be almost universal consensus that Bach is the father of modern music.

In the final analysis, however, Jesus may have had a greater impact on music than Bach. After all, we should not overlook the fact that Christ was the impetus and inspiration for musical development in the centuries before Bach:

While the Roman culture (and the Greeks earlier) excelled in art, literature, and drama, their musical development was rather stunted. In Christ's time, the primary source of music was Jewish worship ceremonies. After the fall of the Roman Empire and during the Middle Ages (for one thousand years, from approximately A.D. 450–1450), music was rather primitive. About the only place music was preserved and pursued during this time was in Christian worship (such as Gregorian chants that were integrated into the liturgy of the Christian church).

In the eleventh century, a Benedictine monk embarked on a project to make it easier for his choirs to memorize hymns. He developed the system for identifying musical notations, which made it possible to compose music in written form. Until then, music was performed only once, and then gone forever. Now it could be written and preserved. Compositions of intertwining melodies became possible. This accomplishment took the music of Western Europe in a different direction from the other music of the world.

Continuing in the Middle Ages, polyphonic music

(harmonizing parts, such as with soprano, alto, tenor, and bass lines) was developed by the choirmasters at the Nôtre Dame cathedral in Paris. Multipart musical arrangements were first created for Christian worship music.

With the advent of the Renaissance (roughly the fourteenth through the sixteenth centuries), music was composed in secular contexts, but its foundation in sacred worship continued. Some of the most famous composers of the baroque period were strongly influenced by their faith in Christ. Antonio Vivaldi (called the "Master of Italian Baroque") was a Catholic priest. And George Friedric Handel dedicated many of his compositions to the glory of Jesus Christ. He stated that his most famous work, *Messiah*—written in just twenty-five days—was composed under divine inspiration.

Even if you discount the Christian influence on music before Bach, it is undeniable that Bach himself considered Jesus Christ to be his divine inspiration. Bach was a committed Christ-follower. One musical scholar has stated that Bach dedicated every single note he wrote to the glory of Jesus Christ. You can find proof on his original musical compositions. On some he wrote the letters "S.D.G." (representing the Latin *Soli Deo Gloria*, meaning "Solely to the glory of God"). On others he initialed "J.J." (for *Jesu Juban*, meaning "help me, Jesus"). Other manuscripts were marked as "in the name of Jesus" with the initials "I.N.J." (for the Latin *In Nomine Jesu*). For Bach, music was about worship. And for him, worship was about Jesus Christ. He could not separate one from the other.

There isn't much to reveal whether Jesus was a musical person. No historical records show him whistling as he walked with his disciples along the roads. You'll never read a verse about him even humming a melody. In fact, you'll only find one reference that he ever sang a song.[79] One song. Not much to qualify him for the historical Music Hall of Fame.

But Jesus didn't have to be a great musician to influence the development of music. Instead, he was the inspiration for others. Some of the world's greatest compositions have been written in worship of the singular, extraordinary person of Jesus Christ. Take any one of those composers away, and you still have the music of the others. But if you take Jesus away, you lose the inspiration for all of them. And that is why Jesus matters.

THINKING ABOUT WHY JESUS MATTERS

- Classical composer Franz Joseph Haydn said that if a composition did not progress, he would "try to find out if I have erred in some way or other, thereby forfeiting grace; and I pray for mercy until I feel that I am forgiven." Based on this quote, consider the spiritual context in which his compositions were written.

- For any of his compositions, how would Bach value his own ability against the value of Christ's inspiration?

- Think about cultures that do not have their roots in Western Europe and do not have a musical heritage as discussed in this chapter. Can you detect a distinct difference in the style of their cultural music? Other than the significance of Christ's role in the music of our Western culture, how do you explain the difference?

And I suppose that if
all the other things Jesus did were written down,
the whole world could not contain the books.

—St. John[80]

CHAPTER 18

LITERATURE

These days we take books for granted. There are so many bookstores and libraries filled with millions of books. But there was a time when only the very rich or very powerful could own a book, because there was no quick and inexpensive way to print books. If you wanted a piece of literature, it had to be copied by hand, usually by monks (and they couldn't exactly knock out a book overnight). Besides that, books were only available in Latin, so unless you passed Latin in high school, you couldn't read it even if you got your hands on a book.

Then came Johannes Gutenberg, a goldsmith and metal-worker who loved books. In the 1440s, he began experimenting with moveable pieces of metal type. By setting up pages of words using moveable letters, he could make many copies of a book at a fraction of the cost and in a fraction of the time it took to copy books by hand.

In 1456 Gutenberg printed his first book, a copy of the Latin Bible. He printed two hundred copies that year, and within three decades, hundreds of printing presses across Europe produced tens of thousands of books and Bibles in many languages. A revolution of printing and literacy had begun. The invention of the printing press made it possible for ordinary people to purchase and read books. Knowledge began expanding at a rapid rate, which has not stopped to this day.

More importantly, thanks to the printing press, knowledge about God and the principles of Jesus have reached every corner of the globe. Since Gutenberg's day, more than six billion copies of the Bible have been printed in virtually every known language. The Bible is by far the most popular book ever written. Even now, although you won't find the Bible on top of the national best-seller list, it is the number one book sold and read each year.

Christianity has often been called "the religion of the book," and you can see why. God could have chosen any number of ways to reveal details about himself to humankind, but he chose to communicate the truth about himself in the book we call the Bible. Not only is the Bible the most popular book in the world, but it is also the greatest piece of literature ever written. Why?

Because the Bible contains the most important story ever written. It's the story of God and humanity from Creation to the end of the world. Even more, it's the story of Jesus, who appears in every book of the Bible—not necessarily by name—but always for who he is: the one sent to show us God's love.

Is it any wonder that more books have been written about Jesus Christ than about any other figure in history? Jesus has inspired some of the most gifted and respected writers of all time. William Shakespeare, John Milton, John Donne, Charles Dickens, Leo Tolstoy, J. R. R. Tolkein, and C. S. Lewis—all of these brilliant writers created world-class literature, much of it filled with Christian themes.

If the Bible is the written Word of God, then Jesus is the Living Word.[81] The writer of Hebrews put it this way: "Long ago God spoke many times and in many ways to our ancestors through the prophets. But now in these final days, he has spoken to us through his Son."[82] Jesus came to show us God and to fulfill everything written about him in the Bible. If all we had was a great book about Jesus—but Jesus had never come to reveal God to us in person—then all we would have is a great book.

But Jesus did come to live among us. It's as if God, the author of the Bible, wrote himself into the plot of his story. Imagine! Anyone who reads this great piece of literature can have a personal relationship with the author. Try doing that with any other book you've ever read.

THINKING ABOUT WHY JESUS MATTERS

- While he walked the earth and interacted with people, Jesus often quoted Scripture (his favorite book was Deuteronomy). Why do you think Jesus placed such a strong emphasis on knowing Scripture?

- Can you think of any great authors writing today who are inspired by Jesus?

- Pretend you are a great author for a moment. What kind of book could you write that would communicate your beliefs about Jesus?

"Then what do the Scriptures mean?
'The stone rejected by the builders
has now become the cornerstone.' "

—Jesus[83]

CHAPTER 19

ARCHITECTURE

*T*he life of Jesus isn't associated with great architectural structures. He was born in a makeshift animal shelter with a feeding trough for his bed. Under the best scenario, his childhood was spent in a modest home (Nazareth, circa A.D. 10–30). And as an adult, it appears the only thing he permanently resided in was his sandals.

If you jumped ahead two thousand years, you might consider it a stretch to say that Jesus had an impact on architecture. After all, there appears to be no cohesive architectural or design theme among modern Christian church buildings. In any given metropolitan area on a Sunday morning, you might find a group of Christians worshiping in a traditional church building with a cross affixed on top of a steeple. But you are just as likely to find Christians in:

- a "megachurch" on a ninety-acre "campus" with buildings that look more like an industrial office complex than a cathedral;
- a public school building (under a short-term lease so no one's sense of separation of Church and State will be offended); or
- a warehouse building (to appeal to those who are curious about Christ but don't want any of the religious trappings).

While facilities may reflect a hodgepodge of design now, it hasn't always been that way. That's why you can't just skip over the intervening two thousand years of architectural developments. For hundreds of years during that time span, architectural advancement was directly attributed to innovations designed to facilitate the worship of Christ.

A.D. 312 is an important date in the timeline of architectural development. That is when the Roman Emperor Constantine the Great legalized—and socially legitimized—Christianity. Before then, Christianity was an "underground" movement (quite literally), as the persecuted Christ-followers hid in the catacombs. But when Christianity became the sanctioned religion of the Empire,

Christians could congregate publicly. Suddenly they needed a place to conduct their worship services.

The earliest Christian meeting places were converted houses called *titulae*. These houses proved inadequate in both space and function. The innovation of the earliest Christian church building, called a *basilica*, has been heralded as one of the most brilliant solutions in architectural history. To facilitate group worship, the design process assimilated and revised various aspects of architectural precedents, such as the Greek temple, the Roman public building, the private Roman house, and the synagogue. The early basilicas resembled large barns, with stone walls and timber roofs. The center portion of this rectangular structure (the *nave*) was supported on columns opening toward single or double flanking aisles of lower height. The variation in roof height permitted high windows in the nave walls.

During the next seven or eight centuries, when little else was happening in Western civilization designwise, Christian church architecture continued to be refined. The floor plans took on the distinct shape of a cross (with the long nave hall being interrupted by side aisles crossing the nave, which was called a *transept hall*). By the eleventh and twelfth centuries, cathedral design defined the Romanesque era with stone arches and vaulted semicircular roofs. Designs shifted in the thirteenth though fifteenth centuries (the Gothic era) with pointed spires on the arches and vaults. In the sixteenth century and after, the Renaissance style predominated as defined primarily by the Roman Catholic cathedrals.

A trip through Europe confirms that sanctuary designs were at the architectural forefront during the past centuries. In a village that otherwise might be filled with only single-story construction of commercial and residential buildings, you'll find a magnificent cathedral rising hundreds of feet into the sky. In what was an otherwise dreary existence, the church was set apart to draw people to the worship of Christ. The sanctuary was intended to be a physical representation of the wonder, peace, and beauty found in Jesus Christ.

By any objective assessment of architectural development and progression, designers who worked their crafts in the name of Christ have made a substantial impact.

Thinking About Why Jesus Matters

- What architectural elements would you include if you were hired to design a building to reflect God's attributes?

- Consider the differences of design among a Christian cathedral, a Muslim mosque, and a Buddhist temple. Why are the architectural styles of these buildings so different?

- Do your surroundings affect you? Does the style of your home and your work environment impact your mood and attitudes? If you are inside a building while contemplating spiritual issues, which type of architectural style might help you focus your thoughts?

Jesus always used stories and illustrations
like these when speaking to the crowds.
In fact, he never spoke to them
without using such parables.
This fulfilled the prophecy that said,
"I will speak to you in parables.
I will explain mysteries hidden since
the creation of the world."

—St. Matthew[84]

Chapter 20

DRAMA

Were Jesus living and working today, he would be a great Hollywood scriptwriter. He understood the power of a story. That's why he spoke in parables. He knew it would be easier for people to understand the point of his message if he could give them a mental picture in real-life terms. So, as any good scriptwriter can do, he used stories of every day people, in everyday circumstances, to illustrate his point. His audiences were enthralled by these stories, so he didn't need canned laughter and sound tracks to evoke crowd reactions.

Many of the parables told by Christ have been depicted on the stage and screen. But the most captivating story was not one that he told—it was the story he lived. Let's face it. His life has Hollywood blockbuster written all over it:

- His mother's teenage pregnancy was shrouded with scandal as she claimed supernatural intervention.

- Angelic proclamations seemed incongruent with the homeless circumstances of Christ's birth.

- Foreign dignitaries who acknowledged his royal lineage visited him while he was an infant.

- Jesus was smuggled out of the country by his parents to avoid the king's death threats.

- As a young man, he was considered a political revolutionary. His radical views won support from those who mistakenly believed he would lead a military overthrow of the Roman government.

- Jesus challenged and criticized the powerful religious establishment.

- He was considered a threat to the government and the religious leaders even though he preached a message of love, peace, and forgiveness.

- A contract was put out on his life.

- Jesus was falsely convicted in a series of phony trials.

- He was given the death penalty although the highest judicial authority admitted that there was no evidence that any crime had been committed.

- Dead and buried for three days, Jesus miraculously resurfaced.

His is a life story of high drama.

Not surprisingly, as civilization progressed out of the Dark Ages and into the early Renaissance, the revival of drama in modern Europe grew out of the Christian church. The dramatic events of Christ's life were portrayed at the religious festivals at Christmas and Easter to mostly illiterate congregations. Although the presentation may have been rough and inartistic, the visual impact was entrancing.

As time passed, these religious plays were performed outside the churches. The scripts were later expanded to include other biblical events. The initial acting troupes were always priests or monks. These miracle plays then began traveling to neighboring towns. This was the birth of the traveling road show featuring the troupes of vagabond actors. Within a couple of hundred years, the profession of acting was entrenched in the culture just in time for Shakespeare.

Christ's life still makes for good box office sales, but it appears that the focus has shifted back to his message. The themes Jesus explained two thousand years ago are relevant and popular today. The parables used by filmmakers and playwrights to illustrate those themes aren't as quaint as the parables of the Good Samaritan or a lost sheep. Now the story lines have the elegance of *Les Miserables*, the complexity of *The Matrix*, and the adventure of *Star Wars*. While the name of Jesus Christ may not be mentioned in these films (except in cursing), they are heavily laced with his themes of redemption, forgiveness, and humanity's struggle with evil.

Jesus Christ's life was the impetus for modern drama. The themes of his message have inspired countless movie scripts and stage plays. Yet Jesus never won an Oscar, a Tony, or an Emmy. He wasn't even nominated. Maybe he should have had a better agent.

Thinking About Why Jesus Matters

- The early church presentations of the events surrounding Christ's birth and crucifixion and resurrection were referred to as "mystery plays." During the Renaissance, the plays depicting the events of Easter week became known as "passion plays." How do you explain these terms?

- Suppose you were given the assignment of warning people in a foreign country of a deadly virus that they could avoid by taking certain sanitary measures. How would you communicate your message if you did not speak the language and had no interpreter?

- Can you identify the plot lines in any movie that deal with themes of redemption, reconciliation, or forgiveness?

PART FIVE

The Sermon of the Mount does not provide
humanity with a complete guide to
personal, social, and economic problems.
It sets forth spiritual attitudes,
moral principles of universal validity,
such as "Love your enemies," and it leaves. . .
the admittedly difficult task of applying them
in any given situation.

—ROBERT J. MCCRACKEN

Why Jesus Matters in
Ethics and Morality

*E*thics are moral values of right and wrong. For generations, most people agreed about what was ethical and what was not. As far as moral values of right and wrong, most people were on the same page. Principles and standards governing human conduct were fairly black and white. There was little gray in the equation.

But then along came the postmodern era of philosophy and the abandonment of absolute truth. By eroding the underpinning of ultimate truth, the foundation for ethics crumbled. Suddenly ethics became a matter of personal determination and the circumstances. Situational ethics was born. Everyone got to set his or her own benchmark of ethical behavior, which could change depending upon the situation. Ethics became a matter of individual preference and personal convenience.

The famous British atheistic philosopher and social critic Bertrand Russell (1872–1970) defined society's egocentric definition of ethics when he said: "I can only say that while my opinions as to ethics do not satisfy me, other people's satisfy me still less." With these words, Russell captured the two prevailing standards of contemporary ethics: First, we each get to decide our own code of ethics; and secondly, we may find that someone else's standard is not acceptable to us.

The approach of situational ethics is diametrically opposed to the teachings of Jesus Christ. He never waffled on moral issues; in his paradigm, truth did not vacillate. Certain behavior was good, right, and true; other behavior was not.

Russell objected to Christ's concept of a fixed morality: "The fundamental defect of Christian ethics," he said, "consists in the fact that it labels certain classes of acts 'sins' and others 'virtues' on grounds that have nothing to do with their social consequences." But Bertrand blew it on that assessment. Jesus Christ proclaimed a morality and ethical context that was all about social consequences over personal preference. When Christ said to "love your enemies"[85] and to "do good to those who hate you,"[86] he was not rattling off an arbitrary checklist of sanctimonious behavior. He was prescribing a perspective of ethics and morality that honored the social order more than a person's selfish motivations.

The next five chapters examine Christ's impact on our concepts of right and wrong. There is no shifting or situational ethics with Christ. For him, relativism was connected with morality. His teachings assert fixed precepts for evaluating what is right or wrong, good or bad, truthful or corrupt. And that is why Jesus matters.

"I came to bring truth to the world.
All who love the truth
recognize that what I say is true."

—Jesus[87]

Chapter 21

TRUTH

A book of this type would have been unnecessary fifty years ago. In all parts of the Western world, Judeo-Christian truths were the basis of prevailing moral consensus. In the past five decades, however, there has been a major philosophical shift in our culture's assessment of "truth." We now live in a *post-Christian* civilization: Biblical precepts are no longer accepted as the basis for establishing moral parameters.

The effect of this philosophical shift goes beyond some antireligious ramifications. Something had to fill the void as the basis of culture's worldview. In the 1960s, it was *existentialism*—a belief that life was meaningless and that ultimate truth was left to each individual's choice. Before long, existentialism morphed into *postmodernism*, a philosophy that rejects any notion of objective, universal truth. In postmodernism, all viewpoints and all beliefs are considered equally valid.

Unfortunately, these culture shifts have not improved our society. Instead, we are left with:

Less social commitment. The rejection of ultimate truth in favor of respecting all viewpoints as valid is paraded under the banner of tolerance. Yet tolerance is not a redeeming social virtue. It merely implies that we put up with each other (i.e., tolerate each other). No overriding moral standard requires that we affirmatively attend to each other's needs (which might have been a shared value in the past but is no longer applicable since moral values are now based on each person's creativity and preference).

Less personal commitment. Less personal conviction exists. There is little sense in debating or fighting passionately for one's ideas and beliefs. If truth is defined on a personal basis, then what is right for you is not necessarily right for someone else. If "your" truth is not applicable to anyone else, it's futile to try to advocate your principles by rational argument.

More abuse of power. Any value imposed on an entire community is an abuse of power. Stanley Fish, a leading postmodernist scholar at Duke University, argues that all statements of principle are really just expressions of personal preferences. Imposing our principles on others in the community, therefore, must be part of a power play. For certain values to be applied within the community, some must exert power to impose their values over the opposing—but supposedly equally valid—values of the others in the community.

There is some irony in the philosophy of postmodernism. Our culture quickly rejects opposing philosophies and beliefs because postmodernism is revered as the enlightened viewpoint. However, how can its proponents assert its truth when it claims no ultimate truth exists? If nothing is true for everyone, then how can postmodernism be universally true?

Postmodernism is being debated as a reliable belief system for life. In the meantime, the rest of us must deal with life's reality. Either there is truth, or there is not. If truth doesn't exist, then our quest to find it is not important. But if truth does exist, we would be well advised to find it. This is a noble search that could have eternal consequences. But where should we look?

The teachings of Jesus Christ stand in sharp contrast to the contemporary void of moral absolutes. Jesus said that God's truth was eternally existent and universally applicable. This is not some obscure form of truth. Jesus claimed that he was the embodiment of truth: "I am the way, the truth, and the life."[88]

Christians since the time of Christ have asserted that an intimate knowledge of Jesus brings an understanding of spiritual truth that puts the physical realm into context. With Christ's truth come certainties that are missing in the paradigm of postmodernism; Christ explained a divine contextual basis for moral absolutes and ethical standards that applies to all people in all circumstances.

Former U. S. President Ronald Reagan once said reality is a stubborn thing. It exists whether we want to acknowledge it or not. The same principle applies to truth. If there is truth in our reality, then it exists and remains applicable even if we choose to ignore it. So we shouldn't adopt a philosophy of postmodernism simply by default. We should knowingly make any decision about the existence—or the nonexistence—of truth. Since postmodernism has little to guide us in the search for absolute truth, we must go to another source for a reality check. Jesus' teachings are an alternative resource in your search for truth.

THINKING ABOUT WHY JESUS MATTERS

- What is the foundation for your personal values?

- What is your basis for making moral decisions? How do you determine what is right and what is wrong?

- Do you believe truths exist that apply to all of humanity? If so, how are such truths ascertained? If not, how can your answer be confirmed?

"And if you do good only to those who do good to you,
is that so wonderful?
Even sinners do that much!"

—Jesus[89]

CHAPTER 22

MORALITY

There are four classic arguments for God's existence. If a skeptic were to ask you to *prove* God exists, you could use these arguments as evidence that God is real, even though we can't physically see him. Here they are:

The God Idea Argument. The fact that every person thinks about God points to his existence. If God doesn't exist, why does everyone—including the atheist—think about him? People may have different ideas about God, but the bottom line is that all people think about some kind of God, who placed that thought in their heads in the first place.

The Cause and Effect Argument. Every effect has a cause. Even the universe, as big as it is, didn't "just happen." There had to be some incredibly powerful first cause that began it. You may ask, "But where did that 'first cause' come from?" That's where God comes in. At the beginning of the string of causes must be something which itself had no cause. By definition, that first cause is God.

The Intelligent Design Argument. Order, harmony, purpose, and intelligence fill nature and the world. Such intricate design did not come about by chance but must have been the product of some great Intelligence that planned and created it all.

The Moral Argument. All human beings have a built-in moral code—an innate sense of right and wrong. We may not always act on what we know to be true, but we know when we have gone against our "conscience." How can people across cultures and circumstances all have a conscience? The answer is that God put it there.

Of the four arguments, this last one sometimes gives people the most trouble, because they see all kinds of evil in the world and wonder, *How could a loving God let all of these bad things happen?*

If morality is built into every person, and all of us know the difference between right and wrong, why do so many people insist on doing wrong? Interestingly, the answer points not just to the existence and the love of God, but also to the necessity of Jesus.

God could have created us so that we could do no wrong. He could have made it so that every person would automatically love and obey him. But that's not what God wanted. Rather than creating a race of robots, he gave us the free will to choose whether or not we wanted God to be a part of our lives. Of course, that free will option has a downside. We can choose to love God, or we can choose to ignore him.

Because the human race has chosen to disobey God, evil fills the world. And because evil fills the world, there is a God. If no evil existed, there wouldn't be a God who loved us enough to let us make our own choices. We have been created in God's image, but we have been given the freedom to reject the very God who made us.

Furthermore, the very idea that we *know* we are making the wrong choices shows there is a God. The apostle Paul argued that even people who have nothing to do with God know "in their hearts" the difference between right and wrong.[90] "They demonstrate that God's law is written within them, for their own consciences either accuse them or tell them they are doing what is right."[91]

So how does Jesus figure into all of this? Why does he

matter when it comes to morality? Jesus matters because we can do nothing on our own to completely satisfy a holy God. To be holy means to be "morally perfect." God is incapable of wrong-doing, but we aren't! We may not always do the wrong thing, but we are incapable of always doing the right thing. Consequently, we need help, which is precisely what Jesus offers.

Once Jesus had a conversation with a rich young man who wasn't all that different from most of us.[92] The way he figured it, his ticket to heaven was being good enough. He was, in his mind, a moralist. So he asked Jesus, "Teacher, what good things must I do to have eternal life?"

Jesus answered, "You can receive eternal life if you keep the commandments."

At this point a smug smile probably crossed the young man's face. "Which ones?" he asked. Jesus answered by reciting a few of the Big Ten commandments—do not murder, do not commit adultery, do not steal, you know the list—and the young man answered proudly, "I've obeyed all of these commandments. What else must I do?"

That's when Jesus looked at him and said, "Sell all you have and give the money to the poor. Then come, follow me." At this the young man's expression changed from one of confidence to sadness. Because he loved his wealth more than God, he walked away from Jesus. His morality went as far as his money.

The disciples, who listened to this conversation, were astounded. If this young moralist, who had everything the world had to offer, couldn't live up to God's perfect standard, then who could possibly have eternal life? The Bible says Jesus looked at them "intently" and said, "Humanly speaking, it is impossible. But with God everything is possible."

Do you believe that? Have you come to the point at which you agree that you can do nothing on your own to live up to what God expects of you? Have you run out of options for living a meaningful, satisfying life? If so, you may be ready to consider the claims of Christ. Jesus lived a perfect life so you don't have to. Jesus satisfied all of God's requirements so you don't have to. You don't need to please God on your own. Jesus has already done that.

Thinking About Why Jesus Matters

- Which of the four arguments for God's existence is most appealing to you?

- Why do you think the problem of evil bothers people so much? Why is it wrong to think that the presence of evil in our world negates the presence of a loving God?

- Even if you were capable of keeping all of the Ten Commandments (Exodus 20:1–17), which no one in history except Jesus has ever been able to do, how do you deal with what Jesus said in Matthew 5:27–28?

"I have given you an example to follow.
Do as I have done to you."

—Jesus[93]

Chapter 23

INTEGRITY

*W*hy doesn't a race car shake apart when it travels over two hundred miles per hour? What keeps the Eiffel Tower from falling down after 114 years, or the Sears Tower in Chicago—at a height of 1,450 feet—from tipping over? The answer to all these questions is the same: structural integrity. These items are designed and constructed to hold up under the pressures to which they are subjected.

There is an analogy with structural integrity to our lives. Each day, to varying degrees, we endure pressure and stress. We find ourselves in difficult situations. The circumstances may tempt us to compromise our beliefs and values. It may not be a big thing, but it will still compromise our principles. Or, it may be something significant that no one else will ever discover.

Whether it is cheating on our taxes, covering a mistake at work, or lying to avoid embarrassment, the structural integrity of our life is constantly tested. How do you come out in such situations? Do you find yourself shaking apart, falling down, or tipping over? Or are you able to stand straight, take the pressure, and endure the consequences because you have internal integrity?

Very few people would deny an interest in integrity. Most people want to have it, but they'll readily admit it is difficult to obtain. It can be easily defined: "The quality or state of being of sound moral principle; uprightness, honesty, and sincerity."[94] But definitions are not easily applied because the circumstances in which integrity is required are always different. It boils down to this: We want to do the right thing—to display integrity in our actions—but we often falter because a technical definition doesn't translate well into the arena of real-life situations. What we could use is a good role model.

This is where Jesus comes in and why he matters. Christ is recognized worldwide as a man who lived an upright life. Not only Christians think this. Jews, Muslims, Buddhists, and atheists will agree that Jesus' lifestyle was moral and principled. There is universal consensus that he led a morally exemplary life. In other words, he had integrity.

Christ's actions and lifestyle have undergone tremendous scrutiny, during his life and in the two thousand years since his crucifixion. During his trial before the Roman authorities, the Jewish leaders attempted to convict him of all sorts of crimes. Yet Pilate, the Roman governor, after listening to the best evidence against Jesus said, "Understand clearly that I find him not guilty."[95] Although Christ was crucified, it was not due to moral failings on his part because, as Pilate said, "[There is] nothing wrong with this man!"[96]

If we want to show integrity in our lives, Jesus Christ is our best role model. We don't have to get hung up on theological arguments about Christ—such as whether he was God or not—on this issue. Regardless of your religious beliefs, you can look to Christ and his teachings as your benchmark for internal integrity.

Christ offered himself as a role model for people to follow. When speaking to his twelve disciples on the night before he was crucified, Jesus said: "I have given you an example to follow. Do as I have done to you."[97] This technique must have worked, because those disciples passed it on. As general guidance for life, the New Testament is filled with admonishments to make ethical decisions using Christ as a role model, such as:

- "Your attitude should be the same that Christ Jesus had."[98]
- "Live a life filled with love for others, following the example of Christ."[99]

Christ can serve as an effective role model for your ethical dilemmas only if you are familiar with him and his teachings. That is not a burdensome task (although many people have devoted a lifetime to that study). You can begin by reading his famous Sermon on the Mount,[100] which can be read in about fifteen minutes. You'll find some familiar principles there, such as "the Golden Rule" in which Jesus said: "Do for others what you would like them to do for you."[101] As a matter of fact, that verse alone is a pretty good reference point when you seek guidance on ethical issues.

Whether designing race cars or skyscrapers, the professionals who build these sophisticated structures first construct a model to ensure structural integrity. To build internal integrity in our lives, we can benefit by using a model. The best model who ever lived was Jesus Christ, and that is why he matters.

THINKING ABOUT WHY JESUS MATTERS

- Who is the most moral person you know? Would it help you to use this person as a role model in making ethical decisions?

- Think of the last time you had to make an ethical judgment call. Would it have helped to ask yourself what Jesus would have done in a similar situation?

- Do you know enough about Jesus to be able to use him as a role model for building integrity in your life?

He [Jesus] does not merely feel compassion,
an emotion that can come and go
and is dependent on outside forces;
he is Compassion.

—THOMAS CAHILL

CHAPTER 24

COMPASSION

*I*t's impossible to overestimate Jesus' impact on the world in the area of compassion. Jesus had more sympathy for others' suffering than any other person who ever lived. Because of his connection to God, he understood that people lived under the curse of sin and evil; because he was also fully human, Jesus personally experienced the pain of people weighed down by overwhelming problems.

We know from history that Jesus healed the sick, raised the dead, cast out demons, and associated with social outcasts. As you read the Gospels, you can't help but conclude that Jesus' compassion motivated his divine power over the physical universe, as well as his authority over the unseen spirit world. Clearly Jesus didn't come into the world just to give us spiritual hope—although that was his primary mission. He also came to give us physical help. Jesus wasn't just the sinners' friend. He was also a champion of the afflicted and the oppressed.

It's important for us to know that the world Jesus was born into was a cruel place. Disease and deformity were common. The Roman government—in power throughout Jesus' time on earth—was an awesome political power. But if you were not a Roman citizen and you were in need, you had virtually no chance of receiving help. If you were a woman or a child, you were a second-class citizen. If you were a slave (there were six million slaves in the Roman world), you were someone else's property. And if you had a disease, people avoided you.

Like a one-man army of compassion and justice, Jesus toppled all of these barriers between the rich and the poor, the free and the slave, the healthy and the sick. He didn't do it by force. He did it by example. Disregarding social conventions, Jesus mingled with society's outcasts and touched the untouchables. In his Sermon on the Mount, he taught that God wasn't there just for the rich and the powerful. If anything, God's blessings were reserved for "those who mourn," "those who are hungry and thirsty for justice," and "those who are persecuted because they live for God."[102]

When he wasn't caring for the needs of the poor, the afflicted, and the oppressed, Jesus was teaching his followers to do so. In his best-known parable, the story of the Good Samaritan, he taught the need to help people who have been beaten down.[103] Jesus even went so far as to equate himself with the sick and the downtrodden. In a remarkable talk to his followers, Jesus said that when we feed the hungry, give clothing to those who have nothing, extend hospitality to strangers, care for those who are sick, and visit the imprisoned, it's as if we are doing these things for Jesus himself.[104] Can there be any greater call to compassion than that?

Jesus' supreme example of compassion has had an incredible impact on our world. The spirit of compassion began with the first-century Christians, who shared their possessions to eliminate poverty[105] and cared for widows by distributing food.[106] While the Roman government executed Christians for their belief in Jesus, the faithful followers of Christ attended to the sick and the poor, even while they spread the Good News message of Jesus.

And this was just the beginning. Since Jesus walked the earth, Christians have set the example in showing compassion to disadvantaged people. Even today, when most people assume it's the government's responsibility to care for the poor and the infirm, organizations founded on Jesus' principles—such as the Salvation Army, World Vision, Habitat for Humanity, and Compassion International—are giving aid and comfort to millions of people in hundreds of countries. Compassion International alone gives food, money, and education to half a million children each year.

Why does Jesus matter when it comes to compassion? He matters because he showed us how to see people as God sees them—humans loved by God.

Thinking About Why Jesus Matters

• Why is pity never the same as compassion?

• Read the story of the Good Samaritan (Luke 10:25–37). Why is this such a powerful parable? Have you ever had an opportunity to be a Good Samaritan? What happened? Has a Good Samaritan ever helped you? How did that make you feel?

• What can you do to get better at showing compassion to others?

This is charity, to do all,
all that we can.

—John Donne

CHAPTER 25

CHARITY

If one word characterizes God, it's *love*. God is holy, God is all-powerful, God knows everything, God is merciful, God is compassionate, God is eternal. But above all, God is love.[107]

To say that God *is* love is not the same as saying that God *has* love, although that is true. To say that God *is* love means that love defines him. He can't not love. God doesn't have to choose to love you or not. He is compelled to love you by his nature. And God doesn't love you because of who you are. God loves you because of who he is.

Although love is never a choice for God, love is always a choice for us. Love is an act of our wills. Oh, we may naturally love something or someone for what they do for us (i.e., give us pleasure), but that love is conditional. Even in our finest moments, when we love others with the kind of selfless love that God expects of us, we can only do so because God loved us first.[108]

This is especially true when it comes to charity. Technically speaking, *love* and *charity* are the same. In the famous "love chapter" in the Bible (1 Corinthians 13), the word *charity* is used instead of *love* in some translations. However, we're going to define charity as actually doing something or providing something tangible for someone in need.

Charity is the logical extension of compassion. When you show compassion to others, you empathize with their suffering. When you are charitable, you do something about it. In a very real sense, the two go hand in hand. Compassion depends on charity to do any good, and true charity must follow compassion.

Jesus embodied the perfect balance of compassion and charity. His compassion for people was so deep that he literally grieved for them.[109] And his compassion turned into charity through his healing touch, in the way he multiplied a single sack lunch to feed a crowd of thousands, and ultimately in the way he sacrificed his life for those he loved. "The greatest love," Jesus told his followers, "is shown when people lay down their lives for their friends."[110] No greater example of charity can exist.

How can we follow Jesus' example in our own charitable work? Certainly we can't heal people, we can't miraculously feed thousands of hungry people, and this business of laying down our lives for others—does Jesus really expect us to do that? In a manner of speaking, yes. Because Jesus has gone before us, showing us by his example how to truly love others and show charity to them, we can participate in healing, feeding, and helping people in need.

In fact, Jesus expects us to do even greater works than he did.[111] Jesus healed many people, but it was a limited number. Through the centuries since Jesus lived on the earth, charitable giving has enabled medical researchers to develop more effective techniques and medicines, resulting in the healing of millions of people. The Gospel records tell us that Jesus fed thousands. But through the generosity of people empowered by God's love, millions are now being fed.

And what about people laying down their lives for others? You don't have to look very far to find examples of those who put their lives on the line to save others.

When you consider what Jesus has done for us, it's easy to see that charity is more than dropping a few coins into the Salvation Army bucket at Christmas, although every nickel helps. Charity is more than serving soup in a homeless shelter at Thanksgiving, although the shelter appreciates your assistance. At its core, charity is an attitude of the heart, born out of compassion, fueled by God's unconditional love, and informed by Jesus' incredible life. Charity puts others' needs, no matter how great or small, ahead of our own.

Thinking About Why Jesus Matters

- Why is it so hard for people to love others uncondi-
  tionally?

- Give an example of someone who has laid down his
  or her life for another. What does that mean to you?

- The blessing of charity is often greater for the one
  who gives than it is for the one who receives.

Part Six

"Love your neighbor as yourself."

—Jesus[112]

Why Jesus Matters in
Personal Relationships

*I*t is time for a pop quiz. Don't worry; it won't be graded, and you only have to answer one word-association question. Are you ready? Here is the question: *When you think of Jesus, what word comes to your mind?*

Was your answer "religion"? That is an understandable response. For many people, Christ represents organized religion. After all, Jesus is the central figure of Christianity, the world's largest religion. And he is recognized as a prophet in the religion of Islam, the world's second largest religion. Jesus also figures in the doctrine of many other religions and cults. So, *religion* is a reasonable answer, but *religion* is not the word Jesus would want to be associated with.

Often times the word *religion* brings to mind rituals, regulations, and man-made rules. Jesus despised the bureaucratic baggage that religious leaders had imposed upon the people attempting to worship God. It was his position that rules and regulations often distract people from God rather than directing them to God. Then, religion becomes a system of "do's and don'ts" in which people worry more about keeping score than about knowing God. This tends to make people hypocritical ("I don't really have to love God so long as I just follow the rules") and judgmental ("I'm better than you because I do a better job at following the rules"). Do you think Jesus was correct in his assessment? Ask anyone who is disenchanted with organized religion. Their reasons usually include criticism about "church people" being a bunch of judgmental hypocrites.

If Jesus had taken our word-association pop quiz, he might have answered with the word *relationship*. In fact, he did. When asked a similar question, he responded that the key to life is a loving relationship with God and a loving relationship with other people. Of course, he said it a little more majestically: " 'You must love the Lord your God with all your heart, all your soul, all your strength, and all your mind.' And 'love your neighbor as yourself.' "[113]

Christ's impact on interpersonal relationships is the theme of the next five chapters. His admonition to build relationships that reflect a "love your neighbor" attitude has huge implications for our society. When applied as Christ taught, his approach has the power to change bitter enemies into friends; to change domestic strife into marital harmony; to dissipate the friction between parents and children and replace it with true love and affection; to forge disinterested neighbors into a caring community; and to help embattled nations find peace. It is not easy, but it is possible. Christ gave us the pattern and the principles to follow. They have proven to be effective when other approaches have failed. And that is why Jesus matters.

"So now I am giving you a new commandment:
Love each other.
Just as I have loved you, you should love each other."

—JESUS[114]

CHAPTER 26

FRIENDSHIP AND LOYALTY

*T*ry to get a mental picture of Jesus walking along Galilee's dusty roads with his motley group of disciples. Mostly fishermen and tradesmen, those disciples must have been a rather rough bunch. They were the equivalent of contemporary longshoremen. This was not a group with delicate manners and fragile feelings. They were the rugged, brawling type of guys.

It is not surprising that the disciples followed Jesus. He was no pasty, frail wimp. Christ had a rare combination of strength and tenderness. He was a tough individual who inspired men with his intensity and attracted women with his compassion. That combination of strength of character and kindness raised the standard for commitment and loyalty among friends for the following generations.

During his last private session with his disciples on the night before he was crucified, Jesus explained a deeper, more spiritual approach to friendship. He said he was giving the disciples a "new commandment" to "love each other." The disciples might have been puzzled over that statement. There was nothing *new* about "loving your neighbor as yourself." That concept had been around since Moses' time.[115] And Jesus had even expanded the application of the concept in his Sermon on the Mount when he said, "You have heard that the law of Moses says, 'Love your neighbor'. . .but I say, love your enemies!"[116] So the disciples must have wondered what was *new* about any of this.

Jesus explained that the new aspect was a deeper under-standing of what it means to love each other. He cranked it up a notch when he told his disciples to love each other "just as I have loved you." For most of us, loving other people can be a shallow and halfhearted exercise, but not for Jesus. Christlike love is not a fifty-fifty proposition in which friends care for each other only to the extent that their kindness and loyalty are recip-rocated. According to what Christ told his disciples, true friend-ship is best defined by sacrifice:

> *I command you to love each other in the same way that I love you. And here is how to measure it—the greatest love is shown when people lay down their lives for their friends.*[117]

Christ's philosophy about love and friendship didn't die with him on the cross. Those concepts were perpetuated by his disciples and in the writings of the New Testament. Ever since Christ's time, the members of every family and community have been challenged to build bonds of love and friendship according to Christ's "new commandment." According to the writings of the New Testament, the ramifications of such love and loyalty include:

Sincerity: "Don't just pretend that you love others. Really love them."[118]

Respect: "Love each other with genuine affection and take delight in honoring each other."[119]

Selflessness: "Don't be selfish; don't live to make a good impression on others."[120]

Humility: "Be humble, thinking of others as better than yourself. Don't think only about your own affairs, but be interested in others, too, and what they are doing."[121]

Unity: "Then make me truly happy by agreeing wholeheartedly with each other, loving one another, and working together with one heart and purpose."[122]

Action: "Let us stop just saying we love each other; let us really show it by our actions."[123]

Perhaps better than anyone else, the apostle Paul captured the essence of what Christ explained to his disciples. Here is how Paul expressed the concept of love as inspired by the life and teachings of Jesus:

> *If I could speak in any language in heaven or on earth but didn't love others, I would only be making meaningless noise like a loud gong or a clanging cymbal. . . . If I gave everything I have to the poor and even sacrificed my body, I could boast about it; but if I didn't love others, I would be of no value whatsoever. Love is patient and kind. Love is not jealous or boastful or proud or rude. Love does not demand its own way. Love is not irritable, and it keeps no record of when it has been wronged. It is never glad about injustice but rejoices whenever the truth wins out. Love never gives up, never loses faith, is always hopeful, and endures through every circumstance. . . . There are three things that will endure—faith, hope, and love—and the greatest of these is love.* [124]

Jesus matters for the simple reason that he announced a concept of love for others that was previously unacknowledged. His teachings in this regard have become the standard to which members of civilization have aspired. Very few manage to maintain that level of love for others; but we are all better off when we at least attempt it. The world is a better place because Jesus gave us a deeper, richer realization of friendship. . .and what it means to be a friend.

THINKING ABOUT WHY JESUS MATTERS

- How do you define love?

- If you asked Christ to critique the definition you just gave, what would he say?

- What would the ramifications of your personal relationships be if love were displayed at only a shallow level?

God places the lonely in families.

—KING DAVID[125]

CHAPTER 27

FAMILY

*C*ivilizations rise and fall, cultures come and go, and even friendships ebb and flow, but one aspect of human relationships endures: the family. Families aren't just one part of society; they are the backbone. Families aren't just important to our existence; they are essential.

Unlike friendships, you don't get to choose the family you are born into. Maybe that's what makes family so special—and sometimes so exasperating. When you choose a friend, you work from a group of preset qualifications that include compatibility, likeability, personality, and visual appearance. With family, you don't get to choose. In a manner of speaking, you are chosen.

And once born into your family, you are a member for life, regardless of circumstances that could potentially alienate you.

Because families are so important to all of us, it would make sense that family matters to Jesus. Yet the four biographies of Jesus give very little information about Jesus the family member. Nor does Jesus talk a lot about families. This has prompted some to conclude that Jesus had little to do with his family, that he was a loner who, when he was with people, preferred to be with his disciples more than his relatives.

While it's true that the Bible offers few glimpses into Jesus' family matters, the ones we do see are powerful and instructive:

Jesus as a boy. The only account from Jesus' childhood is found in the Gospel of Luke.[126] Here we see a picture of Jesus at age twelve, talking with the religious leaders in the temple. His parents, Mary and Joseph, had traveled to Jerusalem for the Passover festival and were on their way back home—without Jesus. In those days families traveled in caravans with other relatives and friends, and evidently they didn't realize Jesus had been left behind (think *Home Alone*). When Mary and Joseph discovered their son was missing, they returned and found him in the temple. Like typical parents, they scolded Jesus for putting them through this ordeal. Even though Jesus had every right to be in his "Father's house," he obediently returned to Nazareth with mom and dad. Jesus affirmed the family structure by submitting to his parents. Jesus knew the fifth commandment—"honor your father and mother"—and he kept it.[127]

Jesus as an adult. Even though Jesus never married, he was fond of families and often spent time in their company. Three of his favorite people were two sisters, Mary and Martha, and their brother, Lazarus. In a famous story, John the Apostle tells of the time Lazarus died.[128] Jesus loved these three siblings, and when he went to Lazarus's graveside, Jesus wept. "See how much he loved him," the neighbors observed. Then Jesus raised his friend from the dead, declaring to Mary and Martha, "I am the resurrection and the life. Those who believe in me, even though they die like everyone else, will live again."

Jesus on the cross. As he hung on the cruel cross, dying for the sins of humanity, Jesus was in agony. Yet he never forgot his mother. Jesus saw Mary, who was in middle age with little means of support, standing near the cross. She was watching the Son of God die, but she was also witnessing the death of her oldest son and primary provider. In a dramatic moment, Jesus instructed his close friend John (the writer of the Gospel that bears his name) to care for his mother. The lesson for us? No matter how difficult our circumstances, we are to care for our family and treat them as God's gift to us.

Jesus valued and honored the family. His words and actions have served as a reminder and a model for cultures and individuals ever since. But his greatest family legacy is not that he set an example for how we should treat our families, but that he made it possible for all people to connect with each other in God's great spiritual family.

A religious leader named Nicodemus once asked Jesus to explain his relationship to his heavenly Father, and Jesus told him that he could also have a relationship with God—if he were "born again."[129] This puzzled Nicodemus, who tried to imagine crawling back into his mother's womb. Jesus explained that this rebirth into God's family is spiritual, not physical. Moreover, spiritual birth is not just for life, but also for eternity.

That's the difference between our earthly families and God's spiritual family, and that's why Jesus matters. With him, the family truly is forever.

THINKING ABOUT WHY JESUS MATTERS

- Think about your own family. What qualities are unique to your family? What do you appreciate most about your family? Have you taken time lately to tell your family members how much you love them?

- Imagine yourself in the place of Mary, Jesus' mother. What emotions must have been going through her mind as she watched her son die in such a horrible manner? How do you think she was affected by Jesus' words concerning her care?

- Why do you think Jesus used the imagery of being born again to describe a spiritual relationship with God?

"You know that in this world kings are tyrants,
and officials lord it over the people beneath them.
But among you it should be quite different.
Whoever wants to be a leader among you
must be your servant,
and whoever wants to be first
must become your slave."

—Jesus[130]

Chapter 28

LEADERSHIP

The research and writings of Robert K. Greenleaf started a major shift in leadership style. Most scholars and sociologists consider Greenleaf (who died in 1990) to have been the leading authoritative voice in management and leadership theory. His treatise *Servant Leadership* was considered groundbreaking when it was published in 1977. Writing in an era of big business egos and excessive executive perks, Greenleaf proclaimed the wisdom and efficacy of leading with a servant's attitude. Imagine that. He suggested that leaders approach their role from the perspective of serving those beneath them on the organizational flowchart.

But Greenleaf didn't have a proprietary claim to servant leadership theory. And he wasn't the first to write about it. Actually, he revived interest in the theory articulated almost two thousand years earlier. Jesus Christ enunciated the concept of servant leadership during his three-year ministry. But in a crowded upstairs room, Jesus acted out a living illustration of the principles he had been preaching. What he did in that room—on the night before he was crucified—has been recorded in history as the best example of servant leadership the world has witnessed. You can read about that night's event in the Bible; you can see it depicted in stained-glass windows; you can hear it preached from pulpits; and you can listen to an analysis of it in lecture halls at major universities. In any discussion of leadership principles, you will inevitably talk about Jesus washing his disciples' feet.

Life in Jerusalem in the first century A.D. was fascinating, but it was also dirty. You couldn't expect feet to stay clean with the combination of dusty roads, open-toed sandals, and no socks. So Jesus and his disciples arrived at the "upper room" for their famous "last supper" with dirty feet. Servants usually would wash the guests' feet. If no servant was present, the lowest ranking person in the social hierarchy would assume the task.

There was apparently no servant in the upper room, although the arrangements had included a towel and a basin of water. Someone should have attended to the task. Social customs dictated that anyone except Jesus should do it. He was the disciples' teacher and mentor. He was the leader of their group. One of the disciples should have assumed the foot-washing duties, but none did (apparently they were preoccupied with arguing about who would be greatest in God's kingdom[131]).

The next moment witnessed the birth of servant leadership. Contrary to all social etiquette, Jesus grabbed the towel, got down on his knees, and went around the room washing each disciple's dirty, smelly feet. With that simple but dramatic gesture, he graphically illustrated some of the most profound principles of effective leadership:

- *An effective leader sees the need.* While others may be too busy thinking about their own interests, a servant leader notices what needs to be done for the benefit of others.

- *An effective leader springs into action when the need arises.* The disciples might have noticed the towel and the basin of water and thought, "It's not my job." But Jesus, the consummate servant leader, saw a job that needed to be done—noticed that no one was doing it—and undertook the job himself.

- *An effective leader acts with humility.* A servant leader considers no job to be demeaning or beneath his or her status. The servant leader never says, "I'm saving myself for the important stuff and will leave the menial work for one of the grunts."

- *An effective leader shows no favoritism.* A leader with the heart of a true servant won't serve some and exclude others. An arrogant CEO may dispense benefits that way, but not a servant. Jesus, knowing that Judas would betray him, may have thought about skipping Judas's feet (or dumping the basin of water on his head). But Jesus displayed the same kindness to Judas that he showed to the other disciples. It is not the prerogative of a servant to show favoritism, and a servant leader won't do it, either.

The story of Christ washing the disciples' feet is counterintuitive. It goes against our natural instincts. For most of us, the concept of leadership is all about the success of someone who rises above to control others. But for Christ, leadership is all about the humility of someone who bends down to serve others.

Servant leadership is radical. It demands that a leader forget about his or her title and get busy grabbing the towel. Leaders have not tried it and found the principles ineffective. Rather, they consider it to be humiliating, so they leave it untried. But Christ's example represents what Greenleaf called "the nature of legitimate power and greatness." It is the standard to which all leaders should aspire.

Thinking About Why Jesus Matters

- Think about the leaders for whom you have worked in a job or a volunteer situation. What was their leadership style?

- When you are in a leadership position, do your natural tendencies reveal a sense of self-importance or the attitude of a servant?

- Is dictatorial leadership more or less effective than servant leadership? Why?

"For the proud will be humbled,
but the humble will be honored."

—Jesus[132]

CHAPTER 29

SUBMISSION

*S*ubmission is a tricky word in our culture. Mostly negative meanings—or often *feelings*—are associated with the word, because on the other side of submission you almost always find authority, and for some reason there's just something about the authority/submission relationship that raises the hair on the back of our necks.

Is it all that necessary to submit to others? Why can't we all be equals? Isn't that what the Constitution guarantees? Even more, isn't that how God created us? Why must one group or class of people—whether bosses, law enforcement officials, or family members—lord it over another class? The answer, while it may be difficult to accept, is not all that complicated. In fact, it makes perfect sense, especially when you see how Jesus fits into the mix.

While he was on earth, Jesus made many claims that surprised and sometimes shocked the people around him. He claimed to be the bread of life.[133] He said he was the light of the world.[134] He claimed that he would come back from the dead.[135] All of these claims were spectacular, but one claim trumped them all and got him killed: Jesus said he was equal to God.[136]

This claim infuriated the people around him, especially the religious leaders who claimed to know God better than anyone else. How could this simple carpenter from an obscure village call himself God? Yet that's what Jesus did.

The problem wasn't so much that the people in Jesus' day weren't expecting God to send a Messiah who would lord it over others. That's exactly what they were looking for. What they weren't expecting was someone who claimed to be God and then proceeded to submit to others, which is what Jesus did. The apostle Paul figured this out: "Though he was God, he did not demand and cling to his rights as God."[137] Why would a Messiah do that? Why would someone who called himself God, who had every reason to lord it over other people, choose to voluntarily submit himself instead? The answer is love.

Jesus loved people so much—even those who opposed him—that he was willing to give up his rights. That doesn't mean he was any less of a person. It doesn't mean his claims were invalid. His example of submission meant that he put others' needs and interests above his own.

That's what submission is all about. The submission Jesus taught and modeled is based on the idea that you treat others the way you want to be treated. Jesus said, "Do for others what you would like them to do for you."[138] That "Golden Rule" is our highest calling. At its heart is the idea that we should voluntarily submit to one another in love, treating each other as equals, wanting the best for one another.

What Jesus taught and modeled about submission had huge ramifications in the ancient world. In those days many "second-class" citizens were forced to submit—usually against their will—to those who lorded it over them. Women were under the complete authority of men, especially in marriage. Children had no rights; in fact, under Roman law, fathers could legally sell their children as slaves. And slaves were treated like property, not people.

Jesus and his followers called upon husbands to love their wives,[139] fathers to treat their children fairly,[140] and masters to care for their slaves.[141] Paul expressed the overriding principle this way: "Submit to one another out of reverence for Christ."[142]

This was truly revolutionary stuff. It still is. When it comes to love and mutual submission, Jesus mattered then and he matters now.

Thinking About Why Jesus Matters

- Why is it so astounding that Jesus came to submit himself rather than to rule? Do you think this prevents or helps people to see Jesus for who he really is?

- In what area of your life do you have the most trouble submitting? How does Jesus help you deal with this issue?

- Why is it always better to serve than to be served? If this is so, why doesn't serving come more naturally?

Jesus loves me! This I know,
For the Bible tells me so.

—CHILDREN'S HYMN

CHAPTER 30

LOVE

*L*ove is a many splendored thing," the song says. Other songwriters and poets have eloquently informed us that love makes the world go 'round, love is all there is, and ultimately, all you need is love. None of us would disagree that love is a powerful force, and many would argue that love is the greatest thing in the universe.

While it's noble to refer to love with such lofty language, we need to define the kind of love we're talking about. Here's what we mean. The love of a man for a woman (or a woman for a man) can be of the noblest sort, and to those two people it may be the greatest thing of all. But what about the love of a man for a dog, a car, or a sandwich? Are those noble loves? Of course not. Those are what C. S. Lewis describes as "Need-loves," as in "I don't have any friends, so I need a dog," or "I need to be seen in that car," or "Right now I need a sandwich."

There's nothing wrong with loving something you need. Most close relationships are based on Need-love. We need the companionship, the warmth, and the love of other people, so we reach out in love. "Our whole being by its very nature is one of vast need," Lewis writes. Even our love for God is based on our need to be connected with the Creator of the universe, who himself is love.

And what about God? What about God's love? Does he need us to love him? No, God's love is of a different sort. It's what Lewis describes as "Gift-love." Because God is love,[143] he can't help but give his love to us, his created beings. He isn't motivated by our loveable natures or our loveable acts (thank goodness). Rather, God is compelled by his own nature to love us. It's always there, even when we don't recognize or acknowledge God's love gift.

God has given us many things that demonstrate his love. We have an incredible world to enjoy. We have life and bodies that function in amazing ways. We have beauty, goodness, and grace. And we have the gift of love itself, enabling us to engage in meaningful relationships. All of these things come from God's love, but none of them can match his greatest love gift of all: Jesus.

Jesus is the literal embodiment of love. For thirty-three years, he lived a life of love that is unsurpassed in human history. Before Jesus came to earth, no one had ever talked about love the way

Jesus did. The Greek philosophers held up the virtues of ideal love, but Jesus talked about the value of practical love. We aren't just to love our friends. Jesus said we should love our enemies.[144] The culture of the day taught a love of convenience and self-interest, but Jesus said we should go out of our way to love the unloveable and those in need. Even Christ's own followers bickered over who would be the greatest in God's kingdom. Jesus taught that the one who serves others in love would be the greatest.[145]

Over and over Jesus expressed his love for people, and all he asked in return is that we love God and love one another.[146] His actions and his words should have been enough to convince everyone that love is all you need. But Jesus had to take one more step to demonstrate the full extent and effect of his love for the world. Jesus had to give himself.

In his letter to the Roman church, the apostle Paul pointed out that you would be hard-pressed to find anyone who would die for someone else, although you might find someone who would give his life for a person who is really good.[147] That's not what Jesus did. He demonstrated his love in an utterly astonishing way. Even though the world hated Jesus, even though his enemies killed him, Jesus willingly sacrificed his life so we could be connected with God in a meaningful and life-changing way.[148]

Jesus is where humanity's need for love and God's gift of love come together. Without Jesus, we can love, but our love is incomplete because it comes from us. With Jesus, we can love, and our love is complete because it comes from God.

THINKING ABOUT WHY JESUS MATTERS

- What is the most loving thing someone else has ever done for you? How did this act of love make you feel, and how did it change your relationship with that person?

- What is the most loving thing you have ever done for someone else? How did your act of love make you feel, and how did it change your relationship with that person?

- Jesus lived his life to show us how to love. Jesus gave his life so we would know how to love.

PART SEVEN

A religion without mystery
must be a religion without God.

—JEREMY TAYLOR

Why Jesus Matters in the Mysteries of Life

*E*verybody loves a good mystery. (Okay, some people just have to know the ending to a story before they read a book or see a movie. But we assume you are among the majority of people who enjoy being surprised.) Mysteries take us out of the ordinary, humdrum, predictable nature of our lives into a world of adventure and intrigue. It's fun and usually rewarding.

We accept and even enjoy mystery when it interrupts our daily lives, but for some reason we balk at mystery when it comes to God. We don't like it when we can't figure God out. We are uncomfortable when things happen that we don't understand. "Explain yourself," we say to God. "Why did you let such and such happen? Where were you when I needed you?"

Sometimes God answers, but often he is silent, causing some people to reject him and his love because they don't have all the answers to life's most perplexing questions. What they are really telling God is this: "I don't think you're doing a very good job of running the universe, so I'm just going to live my life on my own the best way I can, thank you very much."

In these final chapters, we are going to look at some of the mysteries that have puzzled people since time and life began. We may not give you all the answers (we couldn't even if we wanted to), but we will give you the truth, including the truth that the mysteries of God are part of the reality that makes a relationship with him worthwhile.

In this shared experience we call life, it's human nature to want the answers first. But that's not the way God designed it. Rather than showing us everything at once, he speaks to us through the circumstances and the events of our lives, through the joy as well as the pain (and usually more loudly through the pain). And at some point, he speaks to us through Jesus, who offers an answer for our pain—"Come to me, all of you who are weary and carry heavy burdens, and I will give you rest"[149]—and a fulfilling life such as we have never experienced—"My purpose is to give life in all its fullness."[150]

So let's look at some of these mysteries. And if you just have to know the ending to the story, you can find out. All it takes is faith.

Without question, this is the great mystery of our faith:
Christ appeared in the flesh
and was shown to be righteous by the Spirit.
He was seen by angels
and was announced to the nations.
He was believed on in the world
and was taken up into heaven.

—PAUL THE APOSTLE[151]

CHAPTER 31

FAITH

*T*he word "faith" can mean many things. We can have faith in things—for example, that our favorite team will win it all this year. We can have faith in people—believing that the politician we voted for will make good on his promises. We can even have faith in ourselves—"I think I can do it this time."

Although we may consider these to be tangible beliefs, we really have no control over the objects of such faith. The star player on our favorite team could get injured, ruining the chances for a championship. Our elected representative may do the opposite of what he or she promised. And something may happen that prevents us from accomplishing a set goal.

Many people think that faith in God is similar. You can have faith in God, but ultimately you have no control over the outcome, and in the end, there's no way of knowing whether or not everything you believe about God is true. Worse, you really aren't absolutely sure that God is going to be there at the end of your life. So you start to wonder: Maybe all of the God and Jesus stuff is an illusion, invented by someone who wanted to make everyone feel better.

This kind of faith in God is sometimes referred to as "blind faith." The perception is that it's faith for the simpleminded, who have nothing else to carry them through life. It's faith based not on reason and truth, but on wishful thinking. It's faith that has no business in the life of someone who truly wants to know God.

Our faith in a sports team, a person, or even ourselves might be blind, but there's no reason why our faith in God has to be that way. In fact, as R. C. Sproul says, faith in God is the antidote to blindness, not the cause of it. Faith in God is not a weak emotion placed in some unseen and unreal "force," but a strong a dynamic confidence built on the reality of God, who is everything he says he is.

And how can we know God this way? We can know him confidently through Jesus. When his followers asked Jesus the way to God, Jesus replied, "From now on you know him and have seen him!"[152] This statement shocked the disciples, who were always taught that no one can see God.[153] How could this flesh-and-blood person called Jesus, despite his spectacular miracles and extravagant claims, be God in human form? It was a mystery to them, just as it is a mystery to us today.

Jesus claimed to be God in the flesh, God in human form. It's not easy to wrap your mind around this astounding concept. If the first-century followers of Christ, who were around him every day, had trouble believing it, where does that leave us, two thousand years removed from being able to see Jesus in person? What are we to believe? That's where faith comes in, but not blind faith in myths and legends. There is evidence in the form of reliable documents, eyewitnesses, and historical events, which make it possible to have a faith based on reason. All it takes is a willingness to open your heart to the reality of God as seen in the person of Jesus Christ. That's why Jesus matters to you and everyone else who has ever lived.

Of course, you don't have to have every one of your questions answered before you come to faith. You just have to say, as the philosopher William Lane Craig observed: "The weight of the evidence seems to show this is true, so even though I don't have answers to all my questions, I'm going to believe—and then hope for answers in the long run." Maybe that's what the apostle Paul meant when he wrote:

> *What is faith? It is the confident assurance that what we hope for is going to happen. It is the evidence of things we cannot yet see.*[154]

Ultimately your faith is only as strong as the *object* of your faith. Is your faith placed in temporal, tangible things, or is it rooted in the eternal and the intangible? The choice is yours.

THINKING ABOUT WHY JESUS MATTERS

- Why is it so easy for people to place their faith in the things they can see, while believing in things they can't see is difficult?

- Can you think of a time when you believed in something or someone and were greatly disappointed? How did you feel?

- Have you ever been disappointed with God? What did you do about it?

"And why worry about your clothes?
Look at the lilies and how they grow.
They don't work or make their clothing,
yet Solomon in all his glory
was not dressed as beautifully as they are.
And if God cares so wonderfully for flowers
that are here today and gone tomorrow,
won't he more surely care for you? . . .
So don't worry about having
enough food or drink or clothing. . . .
Your heavenly Father. . .will give you
all you need from day to day if you live for him
and make the Kingdom of God your primary concern."

—JESUS[155]

CHAPTER 32

GOD

*W*hat is your concept of God? Do you consider him to be a cosmic killjoy? Or, at the other end of the spectrum, do you think he is more like a celestial Santa Claus? Maybe you doubt that he is interested in humanity, so you view him as a distant deity.

Before Christ, what the world knew of God was primarily through the experience of the Jews and the writings of their sacred scriptures (known today as the Old Testament). God was certainly no one-dimensional being in his dealings with the Hebrew nation, but most of his reputation centered on cataclysmic and punitive events. He kicked Adam and Eve out of the Garden of Eden. He flushed the whole world with a flood, sparing only Noah and his family. He could work a mean plague (take your pick among hail, flies, frogs, grasshoppers, blood, or boils). Sending down fire from heaven was always impressive. And don't forget his penchant for crumbling buildings. Of course, our list would not be complete without famine and other natural disasters. When God made the tabloid headlines with events like those, no wonder many people focused only on God's vengeful nature!

But then along came Jesus. He spoke of God in a completely different light, and from that time, humanity has had a broader, deeper understanding of God's nature.

People's perception of God from a cursory reading of the Old Testament would include knowledge of his power, holiness, and greatness. But the attribute of God most emphasized by Christ was love. It could not be summed up any more succinctly than this New Testament assertion: "God is love."[156]

Love is an overused word in our culture. You *love* your spouse and your kids, and everyone knows what you mean when you say that you do. But you also *love* the members of your extended family, which is often totally different in degree (especially for crazy Aunt Erma). And you *love* the weather in Hawaii, and you've said on more than one occasion that you *love* eating a hot dog at a baseball game. So in our society, saying "God is love" leaves the meaning a little empty.

The same must have been true in Christ's time. When he

expanded people's concept of God, he didn't want there to be any doubt about the nature of God's love for humanity. Jesus didn't want people thinking that God's love could be compared to that of a pet owner (with God loving us in the same way you might love those little wiener dogs).

Jesus amplified our understanding of God by describing unique dimensions of his love:

Benevolence. This is God's concern for the welfare of those he loves. According to Jesus, God unselfishly seeks our ultimate welfare. God's love is an unselfish interest in us for our sake. Jesus explained it this way: "For God so loved the world that he gave his only Son, so that everyone who believes in him will not perish but have eternal life."[157]

Grace. Through this dimension of his love, God deals with his people not on the basis of their merit (i.e., what they deserve), but according to their need. Jesus emphasized that God acts toward humanity on the basis of his goodness and generosity. Jesus taught that grace means that God supplies us with favor even though we don't deserve it. God's love requires nothing from us.

These were radical concepts when Jesus articulated them. And they remain so today. Many people believe they can win

God's favor with their hard work or good deeds (sort of a "brownie points" theology). Either they can't believe or don't want to acknowledge that we have nothing good to offer God, and that we depend upon his benevolence and grace. Such attitudes shouldn't be surprising. One reason the religious leaders opposed Christ is because they were offended by his concept of God. It invalidated the "good deeds" they were so proud of.

Jesus introduced humanity to deeper insights about God's nature. For that reason, Jesus matters, whether or not you believe in God. If you believe in the God Jesus described, then his teachings will give you a greater appreciation for your God. If you are skeptical, then Christ's comments provide you with additional information for your evaluation. If you adamantly deny the existence of any god, then Jesus' teachings on the subject will at least help you understand why the notion of a loving God is so attractive to other people. Wherever you are in the spectrum of belief, the concept of God's love matters.

Thinking About Why Jesus Matters

- How do you define *love*?

- In what ways is God's love different from human love?

- Would your life be any different if your understanding of God's love was based solely on what you know about God from the Old Testament?

In the beginning God created
the heavens and the earth.

—Moses[158]

CHAPTER 33

THE ORIGIN OF LIFE

*A*sk any number of people to list the most important questions in life, and you'll probably arrive at the Big Three: *Where did I come from? Why am I here?* and *Where am I going?* We're going to consider these questions in these last three chapters, and we're going to explore why Jesus matters in each of them.

In a very real sense, these questions are mysteries because we have no way to *prove* the answers are correct. We can't go back in time millions (or billions) of years and actually see the beginning of the universe. Nor can we go forward to the end of time to see firsthand what that will be like. Meanwhile, the question of the meaning of life is about as subjective as they come, or so it seems.

Since we can't know the answers for sure—at least not from a scientific, empirical evidence standpoint—you might be tempted to leave the questions unanswered. That's what a lot of people do. Or worse, they formulate opinions based on feelings and preferences. But is that the way to approach these incredibly important issues? Do you really want to base your life now and your future life in the "hereafter" on what you would prefer? You might prefer a God who in the end will let everyone into heaven, but what if that's not the way it is? You might prefer a God who lets you live with no restraint or consequences, but what if he doesn't see it that way? And you might prefer believing that God had nothing to do with creating the universe, because that means you don't have to answer to anyone greater than you. But what if that isn't true?

We may have preferences, but those have nothing to do with reality and truth. You may strongly and sincerely believe something to be true, but if you're wrong, then all of the belief and sincerity in the world won't make any difference at all. So the best way to approach these life-and-death questions (and that's what they are) is to find out what you do know about these things, uncover the best evidence available, and then exercise your faith, based not on myth or preference, but on truth and reason.

Take the origin of life. The prevailing preference in the world is a belief that the universe came about on its own. But there's a big problem with that belief. Most scientists now agree that the universe had a beginning. They have concluded from various experiments in space that all matter in the universe came about in a single explosion of pure energy, commonly called the "Big Bang." But where did the Big Bang come from? Did that just happen, or did something cause it? It's much more credible to believe that there was a First Cause, which itself had no cause,[159] than it is to believe that our universe appeared by itself. And if there was a First Cause, then only the God described in the Bible, who brought the universe into existence by the power of his word,[160] makes reasonable sense.

What about the amazing design and complexity we see in the world? How do you explain the fact that there are more than forty parameters—and the list is growing—for a "just right" universe? If the size of the solar system, or the age of the sun, or the orbital pattern of the earth around the sun, or the tilt of the earth's axis, or the ratio of oxygen to nitrogen in the atmosphere—if any of these conditions weren't exactly right, there would be no life on earth. The odds of each feature necessary for life occurring together and falling into the required range are incalculably small. In fact, it's impossible—unless an Intelligent Designer is in charge of it all.[161]

And what about miracles, which are the direct result of supernatural intervention in the natural world? Creation itself is a miracle. The way the universe works is a miracle. Closer to home, the disappearance of a tumor diagnosed as deadly is a miracle. How do you explain miracles apart from a supernatural God?

And how do you explain Jesus apart from the miraculous? If Jesus had been a mere human like the rest of us, then his life, his teachings, and his death wouldn't have made any difference. Jesus wouldn't matter. But Jesus did something no other person ever did. He claimed to be God, and then he proved it by rising from the dead. It's not just conjecture. It's not just a story. It's not someone's preference. The resurrection is a fact from history. And if Jesus really did come back from the dead, then we have very convincing evidence that God exists. And if God exists, then it is perfectly reasonable to believe that he miraculously created the universe.

That's why, when it comes to the origin of life, Jesus matters. If there's no Jesus, there's no God. And if there's no God, there's no beginning, no universe, no you.

THINKING ABOUT WHY JESUS MATTERS

- How does believing that God created the universe affect the way you live? How does believing that the universe came about on its own affect the way you live?

- How important is your personal experience when it comes to believing that God created the universe? Does it have any bearing at all? Why or why not?

- Do you think it's too much of a stretch to say, "If there's no Jesus, there's no God"? Could God exist without Jesus?

"My purpose is
to give life in all its fullness."

—Jesus[162]

CHAPTER 34

THE MEANING OF LIFE

*J*esus matters because his teachings give us a fixed point of reference. As a society, our thinking is shifted by current trends, customs, and fads. We alter our approach to life based on the latest theory or philosophy. If you don't think so, just contrast our culture from the 1960s and 1970s (the era of peace and love) with the 1980s and 1990s (when life was all about success and upward mobility). And don't forget the sudden paradigm shift in 2000 and after, with the reevaluations brought about by the burst of the "dot.com" bubble and the terrorist attacks of September 11. Regardless of the attitude *du jour,* the teachings of Christ prevail as unalterable. They are timeless and universal, and people throughout history return to them for guidance when life seems meaningless.

People seldom ponder the meaning of life when they are upbeat. But cheerfulness is temporal and quickly fades in the face of sickness or death, financial adversity, conflict, and the myriad of other stresses we encounter in the existence known as life. When difficulties and misfortune hit, we suddenly question the meaning of it all. Somehow, we intuitively realize that we can more easily endure hardship if we can find a reason behind it or a secret to overcoming it.

Jesus encountered a man who inquired about the meaning of life. The man was a lawyer, so you might suspect duplicity involved with his inquiry. You'd be right to think so, because this lawyer was part of a group intent on trapping Jesus in a technicality of Jewish law. All good attorneys ask a question only if they already know the answer, and the lawyer who questioned Jesus was no exception. Here is how the interchange went:

Lawyer: Teacher, what must I do to receive eternal life? [Okay, we realize that he didn't ask, "What is the meaning of life?" verbatim, but his question is essentially the same. You can't get more meaningful than knowing the secret to life here and beyond.]

Jesus: What does the law of Moses say? How do you read it?

Lawyer: You must love the Lord your God with all your heart, all your soul, all your strength, and all your mind.

And, love your neighbor as yourself.

Jesus: Right! Do this and you will live.[163]

Ever since this short conversation occurred, it has given people keys to finding meaning in their lives. As envisioned and articulated by Jesus, the elements for true meaning and purpose include:

A love of God. Notice that Jesus never specified a particular church or denomination. He didn't include a long list of "do's" and an even longer list of "don'ts." Christ didn't encourage a *religion* with God; instead, he emphasized a *relationship* with God. That makes sense. Meaning in life must certainly follow if you are connected with the wonder and majesty of a supernatural Being. (And a sense of eternity must help, too, but more about that in the next chapter.)

A love for others. Besides a vertical relationship with God, Jesus emphasized our need for a horizontal relationship with others. You may be interested to know that there was more to the story of Jesus and the lawyer. In an effort to clarify what it meant to "love your neighbor," the lawyer asked Jesus, "Who is my neighbor?"[164] (Those attorneys! Always looking for a loophole.) This is when Jesus told the parable of the Good Samaritan, declaring

that everyone is our neighbor and that we have a responsibility to show love to all people.

These two aspects might seem simplistic at first glance, but
a fuller understanding of them (as amplified by the life and other
teachings of Jesus) reveals additional components to a meaningful existence:

• *A purpose bigger than yourself.* This is implicit in loving
  God and loving others. Certainly, a spiritual dimension
  to your life (loving God) and a relational dimension
  (loving others) will take you beyond a self-centered
  world.

• *Intentionality.* Loving God and loving others requires
  more than just intellectually acknowledging their
  existence. We find a sense of meaning in life when,
  without any selfish motives, we actually do something
  that benefits others.

If you haven't found the meaning of life, you can keep
searching. But many people have found the answer in the truth
Jesus proclaimed. Regardless of the changes in our society and
the transitory circumstances of your life, Christ's principles
will remain.

THINKING ABOUT WHY JESUS MATTERS

- What is the meaning of life for you?

- Do you think that there is an overriding "meaning of life" for all people, or can it be different for each individual?

- How is ultimate purpose affected by a spiritual dimension to life? Does the meaning of your life change if you add an "eternal" aspect that comes from faith in spiritual matters? Does your meaning change if you remove that element from your life?

"People soon become thirsty again
after drinking this water.
But the water I give them takes away thirst altogether.
It becomes a perpetual spring within them,
giving them eternal life."

—Jesus[165]

CHAPTER 35

ETERNAL LIFE

One attribute that separates Christ from other famous people in history is his perspective. There have been many world leaders who had foresight and excelled in long-range planning. But none of them had the "long-term view" of things that Christ spoke of. With Jesus, everything mattered in terms of eternity. He viewed life as everlasting.

The people who surrounded Christ didn't see things that way. They focused on the present. They thought about the "here and now," while Jesus talked about the "hereafter." This disparity in perspectives led to quite a bit of confusion, especially between Jesus and his followers. When he talked about establishing his kingdom, they thought he was referring to a military campaign that would overthrow the Roman Empire (or at least free the Jews from Caesar's oppression and occupation of Israel). They considered Christ's references to "the kingdom of God" to be something immediate, physical, and political. They were off, way off.

Those disciples and other followers of Jesus correctly detected Christ's references to change. But Jesus was not referring to a governmental regime change. When Jesus spoke of the "kingdom of God," he was talking about a change in the hearts of men and women. Their hearts needed to be redirected toward God. They had been living for too long under the mistaken belief that they could earn favor with God by following behavioral mandates. When Jesus said he came to set them free from bondage, they mistakenly assumed that he was referring to the Roman Empire. He was referring to the constraints of the rules and regulations imposed through man-made laws of the Jewish religious hierarchy. Christ's battle cry was "freedom," but not in a military sense. It was spiritual freedom.

Critics of Christ often point to his apparent heartlessness. The attacks go something like this:

- If he had supernatural healing powers as he claimed, why didn't he spend more time attending to the sick and handicapped people around him? Why did he often leave the sick and dying and walk away from people who could use his help to regain their health?

- If he could work miracles as he claimed, why didn't he daily provide food for the hungry multitudes? If he could feed five thousand people on one or two occasions, why didn't he do it regularly? Wasn't it selfish of him to withhold his miracles when so many people could have benefited from them?

- If he had supernatural strength, why didn't he lead a revolt and alleviate the pain and suffering that the Jews endured under the Roman oppression? How could he turn his back on his own people that way?

Such criticisms seem legitimate if you have the disciples' short-term perspective. But remember that Jesus was interested in people from an eternal perspective. The New Testament reports that he healed the sick and fed the hungry out of compassion for them, but he refused to be sidetracked from his primary mission of proclaiming the kingdom of God. He was more concerned about humanity's eternal well-being than their temporary comfort. Those he fed were made comfortable until the next mealtime; those he healed were freed of pain for a few years; but his spiritual message involved living with God forever. For Christ, it was a choice between: (a) giving momentary, temporal comforts; or (b) offering never-ending life with the almighty Creator of the universe. Understood in that context, the criticisms seem rather lame.

Christ took a society focused on the immediate and challenged it to think about the eternal. When people around him talked about life, they referred to their current conditions. His concept of life included the immediate but also extended into eternity. He caused people to reevaluate their lives from the eternal perspective.

And that is why Jesus matters today. His challenge to evaluate life from an eternal perspective is as relevant to us as it was to the people in the first century. We can get so caught up in the busyness of life that our perspectives are obscured. We see only what is immediately before us; our long-term vision is measured in years. But Jesus' teachings remind us to broaden our view of the future. His message tells us to define life using an eternal timeline.

Life on earth for seventy or eighty years is inconsequential when measured by the yardstick of eternity. That's why Jesus emphasized that our choices on earth should be made in light of their eternal consequences. Jesus matters because he raises the possibility that there may be more than life as we know it.

Thinking About Why Jesus Matters

- What will happen to you after you die? Will it be a matter of "game over," or will you continue to exist in a spiritual form?

- How much time do you spend planning and thinking about a one-week vacation? How much time do you spend considering the ramifications of eternity?

- If you take Jesus and his teachings out of the picture, would anything be left in your life to remind you to think about eternal consequences?

One day as Jesus was alone, praying,
he came over to his disciples and asked them,
"Who do people say I am?"
"Well," they replied, "some say John the Baptist,
some say Elijah, and others say you are one of
the other ancient prophets risen from the dead."
Then he asked them, "Who do you say I am?"

—St. Luke[166]

WHY JESUS MATTERS TO YOU

*I*t is undeniable and indisputable. Jesus' was the most extraordinary life the world has known. Even atheists and those who are cynical of any spiritual nature in Christ and humanity readily acknowledge the overwhelming impact Jesus has made on our civilization. The famous historian—and self-professed skeptic—W. E. H. Lecky conceded the importance of the life of Jesus Christ with this statement:

The character of Jesus has not only been the highest pattern of virtue, but the strongest incentive in its practice, and has exerted so deep an influence, that it may be truly said that the simple record of three short years of active life has done more to regenerate and to soften mankind than all the disquisitions of philosophers and all the exhortations of moralists.

But just as his impact cannot be denied, we can't ignore the controversy he has generated. No individual has caused more debate than Jesus Christ. For such a central figure in history, there is little consensus about him. Jesus has split public opinion about himself into two divergent opposing camps. It seems that either he is respected and revered, or he is despised and denigrated.

So what is all the fuss about?

Is it about his *morality*? No! He is universally recognized as the greatest moral teacher of all time. No one argues with his admonitions on interpersonal relationships or his concepts of right and wrong.

Is it about *the legitimacy of the miracles*? Not really. Whether they were supernaturally caused or were a grand illusion is not what impassions the debate.

Is it about *the fact or fiction of the resurrection*? Nope. It didn't appear to be the issue that fueled the controversy in the first century A.D., and it doesn't appear to be the center of the dispute now.

There would be no controversy if Jesus was merely: (a) a

respected ethicist; (b) with a knack for supernatural theatrics; (c) who appeared to defeat death; and then (d) disappeared into thin air without a trace. Those listings in his biographical profile would make him famous and mysterious, but they wouldn't put him at the center of the world's greatest debate.

The controversy about Christ centers on his *theology*. In the holy hullabaloo that swirls around Christ, some consider his theological doctrine to be his greatest attraction; others consider it to be a grand offense. The different viewpoints are understandable considering that he claimed to know God.[167] Beyond that, he claimed to be God.[168] And most controversial of all, he claimed that his death on the cross was the only way a sinful humanity could be forgiven by God and experience eternal life.[169]

Any honest study of the life of Christ will embroil you in the debate. It is not possible to look only at the extraordinary part of Jesus without dealing with the controversial part. His teaching, miracles, and resurrection are integrated with his theology. His promises for a life of truth, peace, and meaning were all based on a belief in him. . .not just an intellectual assent of his existence, but a faith that he was the sole solution for humanity's spiritual void.

Every person must take a side in the controversy. You must decide if Jesus was just a good man, or if he was the God-Man. Your decision will take you far beyond knowing why Jesus matters. On a more important level—a very personal level—you will know why Jesus matters *to you*.

NOTES

1 Galatians 4:4

2 John 3:16

3 Mark 2:5

4 John 14:7

5 Mark 9:23

6 John 20:25

7 John 20:27

8 John 20:29

9 Isaiah 9:6–7

10 John 8:36

11 Romans 8:1–2

12 Galatians 5:1

13 Isaiah 11:1–5

14 Genesis 3:15

15 Luke 1:31

16 Matthew 1:21

17 1 Corinthians 12:13

18 Genesis 1:27

19 John 3:16

20 Matthew 18:14

21 Mark 10:14

22 Luke 8:1–2

23 Ephesians 5:25–28

24 Philemon 10, 16

25 Matthew 7:12

26 John 3:16

27 Ephesians 1:9, 10

28 John 13:34, 35

29 Matthew 22:39

30 Matthew 5:44

31 Luke 12:34

32 Luke 16:13

33 Mark 10:23

34 Matthew 25:14–30

35 Matthew 6:31–33

36 Exodus 20:17

37 John 3:27

38 Matthew 25:23

39 1 Corinthians 10:31

40 1 Timothy 6:18

41 Luke 12:48

42 Luke 12:33, 34

43 John 14:6

44 John 3:16

45 Matthew 11:28

46 Luke 10:25–28

47 Matthew 7:28, 29

48 John 3:2

49 Matthew 7:28, 29

50 Mark 12:37 KJV

51 Matthew 19:14

52 John 14:6

53 John 7:16

54 Colossians 1:16

55 John 2:6–11

56 Mark 4:35–41

57 John 11:38–44

58 Luke 19:10

59 John 8:12

60 John 1:9

61 Romans 2:14

62 Genesis 1:28

63 John 3:16

64 Genesis 12:1–3

65 Exodus 3:8–10

66 John 14:1–4

67 Matthew 15:30–31

68 Matthew 28:19

69 Matthew 28:19

70 Acts 1:8

71 John 2:23

72 John 10:30

73 Colossians 1:17

74 Philippians 4:8

75 Genesis 1:31

76 Colossians 1:16, 17

77 Romans 8:20–22

78 Colossians 1:18–20 *The Message*

79 Matthew 26:30

80 John 21:25

81 John 1:1

82 Hebrews 1:1, 2

83 Luke 20:17

84 Matthew 13:34–35

85 Matthew 5:44

86 Luke 6:27

87 John 18:37

88 John 14:6

89 Luke 6:33

90 Romans 2:14

91 Romans 2:15

92 Matthew 19:16–26

93 John 13:15

94 *Webster's New World College
    Dictionary* (4th ed.)

95 John 19:4

96 Luke 23:4

97 John 13:15

98 Philippians 2:5

99 Ephesians 5:2

100 Matthew 5–7

101 Matthew 7:12

102 Matthew 5:4, 6, 10

103 Luke 10:25–37

104 Matthew 25:35, 36

105 Acts 4:34

106 Acts 6:13

107 1 John 4:8

108 1 John 4:19

109 Matthew 23:37

110 John 15:13

111 John 14:12

112 Matthew 19:19

113 Luke 10:27

114 John 13:34

115 Leviticus 19:18

116 Matthew 5:43–44

117 John 15:12–13

118 Romans 12:9

119 Romans 12:10

120 Philippians 2:3

121 Philippians 2:3–4

122 Philippians 2:2

123 1 John 3:18

124 1 Corinthians 13:1–13

125 Psalm 68:6

126 Luke 2:41–52

127 Exodus 20:12

128 John 11:1–44

129 John 3:3

130 Matthew 20:25–27

131 Luke 22:24

132 Luke 14:11

133 John 6:35

134 John 8:12

135 John 2:15–22

136 John 10:30

137 Philippians 2:6

138 Matthew 7:12

139 Ephesians 5:25

140 Ephesians 6:4

141 Ephesians 6:9

142 Ephesians 5:21

143 1 John 4:8

144 Matthew 5:44

145 Mark 9:35

146 Matthew 22:37–39

147 Romans 5:7

148 Romans 5:8–10

149 Matthew 11:28

150 John 10:10

151 1 Timothy 3:16

152 John 14:7

153 Exodus 33:20

154 Hebrews 11:1

155 Matthew 6:28–33

156 1 John 4:8

157 John 3:16

158 Genesis 1:1

159 Exodus 3:14

160 Hebrews 11:3

161 Psalm 19:1–6

162 John 10:10

163 Luke 10:25–28

164 Luke 10:29

165 John 4:13–14

166 Luke 9:18–20

167 John 5:24

168 John 12:44–45

169 John 11:25–26

BRUCE BICKEL AND STAN JANTZ

*B*ruce Bickel is an attorney and motivational speaker. He lives in Fresno, California, with his wife, Cheryl. Stan Jantz is a partner in a community-building software development company. Stan and his wife, Karin, live in Southern California. Together Bruce and Stan have written more than forty books together, including the best-selling *God Is in the Small Stuff* and *Knowing the Bible 101*.

Are you interested in further reading on the societal impact of Jesus Christ? The authors found the following resources helpful and heartily recommend them to you:

What If Jesus Had Never Been Born?:
The Positive Impact of Jesus in History
by D. James Kennedy and Jerry Newcombe

More Than a Carpenter
by Josh McDowell

A Case for Christ:
A Journalist's Personal Investigation of the Evidence for Jesus
by Lee Strobel

Mere Christianity
by C. S. Lewis

———————————————————

Perhaps you would like to:

Schedule the authors to speak at an event;
Learn more about the other books they have written; or
Contact them with your questions and comments.

You can do so by:

Mail: Bruce Bickel and Stan Jantz
                          c/o Twelve Two Media Group
                          P.O. Box 25997
                          Fresno, CA 93729-5997

E-mail: info@TwelveTwoMedia.com

Web: www.TwelveTwoMedia.com